This is a book of self-discovery and enlightenment. It's about other people's experiences in situ. It's about predicaments that happened, some by design some by default. The experiences nevertheless were very real. It's about how each individual "took charge" of their life, which in reality is what everyone should do. It's often about going against the odds, yet in doing so a far more intimate reality emerges of joy.

The stories are the feedback from shows and talk programmes that have been broadcast on radio in over 180 countries. Many of these countries have no endemic "social or lifestyle" content available, even in the UK or USA much information isn't so readily available because of the narrowness of organisations, taboos, religious biases, incompetence, historical cultural ideology, fear, media hype and negativity, ineptitude, embarrassment and much more.

Published by
Filament Publishing Ltd
14, Croydon Road, Beddington,
Croydon, Surrey CR0 4PA
+44(0)20 8688 2598
www.filamentpublishing.com

The Wisdom of Aunty Bronwyn
as told to John Rushton

ISBN 978-1-915465-61-0

© 2025 John Rushton

The right to be identified as the author of this work has been asserted by John Rushton in accordance with the Designs and Copyrights Act 1988

All rights reserved
No portion of this work may be copied by any means without the prior written permission of the publishers.

Printed in the UK and the USA

AGONY LETTERS

Extracts from Aunty Bronwyn's postbag

"After your broadcast I just stopped literally following anyone and everything, concentrating on what I wanted and all of a sudden, to have a life again. Everything else I lost interest in, and I was able to think more clearly and concisely too and develop what I wanted from life.

I stopped following all the celebrity rubbish, predominantly silly people made famous many of whom were constantly in rehab and I used to read about that as if it was important news, who cares? If you don't respect yourself and place importance on yourself as you say Aunty Bronwyn, then there is little hope of anything good ever happening, and you get hurt just so much easier. That's all changed now thank goodness."

"Thank you, Aunty Bronwyn for just saying what was the obvious but you know sometimes you have to hear it from someone else for it to register. I'm sure your shows have helped many more people. Best Lew.

AUNTY BRONWYN SPEAKING TO JOHN RUSHTON

"Aunty Bronwyn, thank you for getting me to open my eyes, I was wallowing in the "poor old me syndrome" another of your sayings for so long I couldn't see the love around me. Thank you so much for your shows life is so much better now. Kind wishes Ellen."

"You were right in that everyone who procrastinates or doubts hardly ever listens to themselves, they look outside of themselves as to what might happen elsewhere or permutations that no one can control thus they get so lost. It's not easy to just switch from one mode of years of expertly getting nowhere to saying yes or no and moving on in an instant, but it has made life better for me. I no longer get so tied up within myself, and I'm getting far more confident at making decisions based upon what's good for me.

Thank you Aunty Bronwyn I'm now a loyal fan of yours"

"Aunty Bronwyn, life has picked up considerably now because as I'm open to new things and events they present themselves to me. Before I couldn't see them for looking inwards and thinking "poor old me, what's to happen". I was the cause of my own dismay.

Thank you, Aunty Bronwyn you have really laid down the information for me to get life rolling again and it has. Thank you again."

Reader's Letters and calls to
"THE AUNTY BRONWYN RADIO SHOWS"

She knows all the answers!

WHAT IS THIS BOOK?

As the title depicts, it's an anthology of very brief aspects (not complete stories) of people's lives from all genres over the world over, who have had a problem with themselves regarding other people, no matter who they are.

The chapters point out just how quickly whatever situation you are in, you can suddenly take charge with "I'm not standing for this any longer", that's it. No great procrastination, no lengthy game playing, nothing, you just "take charge" and from that moment everything changes.

The brief chapters depict the background and story / situation, the rest is just that mental flip from being a part of the mayhem to being in control of it, so quickly, no excuses, nothing, that's it.

Not only does your life change but everything around you automatically changes, your mind changes, your thoughts change, your feelings change, your future changes, how you view life and everyone around you in it changes, your resolve changes, your stamina changes, you see immediately great potential, great outcomes, all the suppressed aspects of life are now yours for the taking, just greatness. You see others who once suppressed as helpless and pathetic which of course they are as you have in one fell swoop taken all their power away from them. Their screams and shouts are now on the other foot, that helplessness they are experiencing for themselves.

It doesn't mean for one minute that you are not nervous or that at that moment everyone will not be in shock, that is of no importance, this is about you, they can look after themselves. It doesn't mean either that the immediate future will perhaps not be easy, but it does mean that breaking free from the selfish shackles of others and any man-made constraints such as religions, customs, traditions, oppressions, etc, just falls away, and eventually fades into insignificance as your new fantastic life, the one which is totally yours has at last everything that you want on offer.

How you view life and your attitude depict totally how life will be for you.

Introduction

The following are a small selection of letters picked from our mailbags over the years from listeners from many parts of the world who have written in in response to topics that have been broadcast via radio, internet or via our App and website. You don't have to have had to listen to the shows to see how people changed their lives or turned around what was troubling them as it is self-evident in their responses. The letters cover an amazing array of situations which depict life as it is. What these letters do show however is that our basic emotions cover a massive range of permutations in how we deal with the very same things and the amazing diversity of options we as individuals place on them in doing what we do. The content which is predominantly positive (because few write with negative comments with the exception of those who are disturbed or just pathetic) is done so without moral bias or legal stance or judgment.

The success of the Aunty Bronwyn Show has been down to three main elements, the frankness and down to earth comments which are very soluble and thus easy to understand. The fact that Aunty Bronwyn has herself lead a very rich international life ranging from the very low low's, to the dizzy heights of affording a very comfortable lifestyle. Even now her motto is "never ever give up". The third thing which has raised her notoriety is the humour. No matter where you are or who you are humour raises the game and takes out the drudgery, the mystic and all the psycho-babble which at times adds heavily to the complexity of what to do and the comprehension of same.

Over the years her audience has increased, and the information and her thoughts are now broadcast to over 180 countries. For many in these countries such advice is the only source that can be received via radio or the internet on topics of emotional value as it is either taboo or clouded in archaic or religious stupidity. The broadcasts have brought considerable comfort and made bearable burdens brought about by ignorance and frustration and appeased many a mental health situation developing.

The introduction of the Aunty Bronwyn App has made a great difference in that it's ever increasing interactive element allows people to hone-in, not only to current broadcasts but past topics where they may wish to seek information or thoughts on predicaments should they find themselves in a quandary at any time. The shows are downloadable for any phone or tablet platform as well as your PC / laptop. It's also very comforting and nice to know that what you are going through others somewhere have gone through the same situation or circumstances no matter how unique you think your circumstances are. Aunty Bronwyn encourages people to write or email in with their thoughts on the shows on how they have overcome events in life including the funny parts too, as we can all share in the laughter or fun together. It is this sharing that produces a camaraderie and enhances the love content in our lives as it really does touch those inner parts that at times are so desperately in need of a human touch to bring a degree of reality and warmth to what may otherwise be cold and lonely.

What the letters received do show is a dichotomy of human nature where on one side there is a strong and humane element of love and compassion. And on the other hand, there is a gross ignorance, arrogance, selfishness and fear of something that they can't understand. The enlightened see the bigger picture whereas those who are less informed and possibly both narrow minded and bigoted see only their side which throws them by default into a chaos that they even themselves can't control and thus cause masses of unnecessary upheaval, pain and undue anger, often referred to as cognitive dissonance.

The letters are inspiring and more often than not they just outline that the simplest of things to say or do or just let go of are what makes everything come together. All the consternation of trying to do something but not wanting others to get upset or whatever it is, is not what you are about in life. You have no contract with anyone including your parents to lie or hide the truth from them making your life a misery. Parents or others getting upset is for them to get to grips with not you to play games around. You are the most important person in the world and if you can't look after that person who can, as no one can ever live within your mind. Being nice or trying to be a good person doesn't come into the equation in living a good life in fact those that get easily upset are usually far from being nice and kind themselves, they get upset because something has ruffled their thinking and narrowness and has nothing to do with you or indeed any love element. Being upset – for many - is totally selfish and self-centred in as much as "how dare you upset our/my lives" as opposed to feeling and seeing the compassion that's needed. If you fear what your parents say or think they will never get over it, it is actually a fear of your own that they may just not love you as you think you are loved, and that in turn would tear you up which perhaps you are not ready for. But that is still no excuse to pontificate or procrastinate.

AUNTY BRONWYN SPEAKING TO JOHN RUSHTON

One of the most important love aspects of any parent is that their child or children should be happy, what more could they ask for, after that everything else is secondary. If this is not the case or that parents have personal ulterior motives or worse still conditions on their children, then there is something drastically wrong and love is not a key element in their selfish thinking. Conditioned cultures, greed, evil religions are usually the dark forces at work in such thought processes.

How we view life however, is all down to perception. It is also a reflection of how we feel about our life, our love and our future too. Life isn't one sided and we can't admonish personal responsibility, nor can we outsource our lives and love to anyone else because it resides in us. If we falter on respecting ourselves we open the door to a myriad of negative feelings, fears, mishaps, grief and unhappiness.

Never let the 'mind gremlins' or fear take a hold, you are stronger than you think. If you hold-back because "others" may not like it or get upset then you are not being honest with yourself, the situation, your feelings, them, life and everything else. It is a choice that you have to make, but it is always a worthwhile choice even if your parents have been domineering for years on end and you suddenly told them or anyone else the real truth and how you felt or feel.

In a similar vein, those around you must love you for who you are and that even includes those in a work environment. You don't have to like everyone on planet earth, it is physically impossible and likewise not everyone will like you – for whatever reason. Never indulge in "political correctness" that is failure stamped throughout; you have a right to your opinion, what others think is their opinion and none of your business. Provided what you say comes from a good place even if it is quite strong you are entitled to say it. Never hold back because others don't think the same, creativity and breakthroughs and happiness evolve by those who think differently. Don't ever lower yourself to the level of others and don't take for granted that just because someone has a seemingly "good" position in life they know better, it's often where evil lies as does smugness, complacency, arrogance and very personal hidden agendas and some are just too genuinely "long in the tooth and past it".

The letters also outline the vast complexity of the human condition and how individuals suddenly find themselves in a place not of their initial choosing.

How life, society, the law, people, cultures, ideologies, religions all intermingle often causes more harm than what was or is the base of the problem. Getting to grips with our lives and problems is paramount for if we can't then we will by default enter a rollercoaster ride without brakes and that will inevitably change whom we are, sometimes irrevocably for the worse or scar us to the extent that the edge of happiness is forever tarnished.

The letters by and large are random in content, however where there are parallels or similarities they have been grouped together to show that there is always another side to what most people think or even know about and how complex life can be, often developing out of very simple motives or situations. Many a "scenario" happens without forethought or design, circumstances just stack up and before you know it something that had never crossed your mind has developed.

The Aunty Bronwyn Shows and its sister broadcasts have broached topics that are at times regarded as taboo, however they are very real and exist and everyone needs some degree of understanding and ground. There is a big difference between what happens by default and by design, where one goes out of one's way to impose a degree of hurt or definition on others in society. Much of the angst that is caused is not by the parties involved but by those on the periphery who by their own volition, ignorance, bias, small mindedness, lack of love, bigotry, ego, arrogance, media fodder for a story, etc, feel that to speak out and comment elevates them as people of standing whereas in reality it shows them as quite the opposite, and it changes nothing.

This is the first book in a new series that identifies life as it is combining, video, television, radio and internet interaction with real people who are part of the subject matter and are not just bland statistics overwritten by some research author. Enjoy.....

> ***Wise men don't need advice.***
> ***Fools won't take it.***
>
> ### *Benjamin Franklin*

Table Of Contents

Preface		5
Introduction		7
Table of Contents		
Index		13
Chapters		
1	Failing Relationship	19
2	Single Mother, With The Teenage Boys	21
3	Aggressive Manager At Work	23
4	Domineering Religious Family	25
5	Mixed Race / Multi-Cultural Marriage	26
6	University Student, Going Her Own Way Against The Family	28
7	Incest / Rape In Religious Family	30
8	City Tycoon Has Health Shock And Mid Life Career Change	32
9	Married Woman Finds Lesbian Partner	34
10	Gay Asian Boy Stands His Ground	36
11	Italian Shunned By Jealous Parents Over Daughter's Death	38
12	Young Gay Lover Copes With Elder Partners Death	40
13	Elderly Widow Comes To Terms With Friends Who Show Up On Death Of Husband Only	42
14	Overcoming Difficult Family Relationships	44
15	Loner And Swat Loses Best Friend In Suicide	46
16	A Dear Aunt Dies Leaving Distraught Niece	48
17	Coming To Terms With Wife's Death	49
18	Finding Happiness Again After Mother Dies	50
19	Twin Eventually Gets Over His Brother's Needless Death	51
20	Brother And Sister Lose Parents But Build Life Again	52

21	Getting A Relationship Back On Track	54
22	Breaking That Cultural Bubble	55
23	How An Orthodox Jew Finds Real Love By Leaving Home	56
24	Indian Girl Refuses To Be Married Off By Parents	58
25	Getting A Life Again After Husbands Affair	60
26	Incest – Love Or Sex?(1) Brother And Sister In A Relationship	62
27	Incest – Love Or Sex?(2) Brothers In A Relationship	64
28	Incest – Love Or Sex?(3) Sisters In A Relationship	66
29	Incest – Love Or Sex?(4) Father And Daughter	68
30	Incest – Love Or Sex?(5) Two Sisters And A Male Partner	70
31	Unmarried And Unwanted Pregnancy Second Time Around	72
32	After The Failed Suicide Attempt	74
33	When You've Failed All Too Often	76
34	Finding A Job And Re-Evaluating Life	78
35	Our Mental Health	80
36	Taking Ownership Of Your Life	82
37	Love And Religion	84
38	Dysfunctional Families	86
39	Why Am I Bullied?	88
40	Drugs The Pit To Nowhere	90
41	Loneliness Is It A Choice Or Not?	92
42	Saying No - Often A Difficult Thing To Do	94
43	Stop Waiting For Approval	96
44	Mental Health – Middle East	98

45	My Disability – My Life	100
46	Death – When It Hits You Hard	102
47	Where Success Lies – Within You	104
48	Families Are Strange – Not Being Equal	106
49	Middle Aged And Confused	109
50	Older / Younger Gay Relationship	111
51	Infidelity / Unfaithfulness – A Step Too Far (1)	113
52	Infidelity / Unfaithfulness – A Step Too Far (2)	115
53	Addicted To Sex - Male (1)	117
54	Addicted To Sex – Female(2)	119
55	Permission, Approval, Validation(1)	121
56	Permission, Approval, Validation(2)	124
57	Choices (1)	126
58	Choices (2)	127
59	Normal (1)	129
60	Normal(2)Depression	131
61	Getting In With The Bad Crowd Two Black Boys	133
62	Hopelessness(1) Rich Kid	135
63	Hopelessness (2) Poor Kid	137
64	Expectations	139
65	Deep Disappointment	141
66	The Common Denominator – You	143
67	Love - Life	145
68	Love - Gay	147
69	Love - Elderly Pensioner	149
70	Love - Commercial	151
71	Respect (1)	153
72	Respect (2)	155
73	Past Responsibilities	157
74	Living In The Past	159
75	The Placebo Effect – Encouragement	161

76	An Affair With My Friend's Father (1)	163
77	An Affair With My Friend's Father(2)	165
78	Middle Aged Wife Crisis	167
79	Daughter And Parents Domineering In Old Age	169
80	When Religion Can Take Over	171
81	Happiness – Why Aren't I Happy	172
82	Loneliness	174
83	Failure – Not As Bad As You Think	176
84	Political Correctness	178
85	Anger - Serving No Purpose	180
86	My Secret World (1) What's Your Fetish?	181
87	My Secret World (2) Bondage And The Rest	183
88	On The Game	185
89	You've Got To Be In It To Win It	187
90	The Feeling To Be Needed	188
91	Letting Go	190
92	The Future Is What You Make It	192
93	Changing Life – Mid Term	193
94	I'm In Need Of Love	195
95	Being Rejected And Turned Down	197
96	Coping With Difficult People	199
97	Creative Frustration	201
98	Don't Waste Time On Insignificant People	203
99	No Sex Relationship	205
100	I Was Losing My Self Esteem	207
101	Doubting Myself	209
102	Married And White. Black Affair. Child On The Way.	211
103	Jealous Brother And His Wife	215
104	Caught My Brother In Bed With My Girlfriend	217
105	I'm Hiv+ The First Time I Had Sex - Once	219
106	Wife 33, Three Children, Dies Of Cancer	221

107	Getting Lost In Life	223
108	Irresponsible And Weak Parents	225
109	Being A Failure	226
110	Coping With Difficult People	228
111	Shyness And Timidity	230
112	Gay Muslim - Inbred Hatred - A Family Divided	232
113	Dysfunctional Childhood Laid To Rest	234
114	Whinging & Political Correctness Taken Care Of	236
115	Unemployed And Feeling Undervalued	238
116	Changing The Way You Look At Life	240
117	Four Sisters – Three Slim And Fat Me	242
118	Jewish And Gay – The Good And Not So Good	244
119	It's My Life Not Yours	247
120	Listening And Talking	250
121	Life's Angst	252
122	The Tale Of Having Endless Boyfriends	255
123	Life Hysteria	257
124	Am I Bi-Sexual Or Am I Playing The Field?	259
125	Breaking Up The Relationship	261
126	When Life Long Friends Fade Away	264
127	Toxic Friendships	266
128	Those Mythical Family Lines – An Asian Story	268
129	Black And Gay	270
130	When Anger Takes Over	273
131	Don't Compare Your Life – It's Yours	276
132	Jewish Boy – Muslim Girl – Happy Family	278
133	The Mental Health Conundrum	281
134	I Like Being Single	283
135	I Am Society	285
136	The Power Of Love - Disownment	287
137	Breaking Free – A Girl's Story	289

138	Toy Boy Or True Love?	292
139	"Daughters" And "Daddies" - Young Girl And Older Man	295
140	Don't Be Afraid To Disappoint	298
	End Chapter	301
	Contact Details	303

1

FAILING RELATIONSHIP

I have a letter from Leon who says. Aunty Bronwyn My relationship with my partner has for many reasons gone sour. I've been trying to bring it round yet again, but it seems futile. I've been wishing and hoping for better things but deep down, living in dread at the same time.

A friend of mine asked me over and he said listen to this, it was your show on Taking Ownership". And suddenly everything became clear. I have a life and I don't need to continue living in a sad state regardless of how it has come about.

I thought carefully what you said, about me thinking about me in the equation and why it wasn't working out, and to separate the ideals of what I would wish to happen, as opposed to what is really happening. I eventually approached my partner, and whilst it was not easy – for both of us - it did all make sense.

Hearing your voice in my mind gave me the courage to put succinctly how I felt, what I would have liked, but how it really is. She listened, went very quiet and I almost froze in the silence, then she looked at me quite shocked but almost relieved herself, and reluctantly agreed. It was a momentous cathartic moment, it was difficult because at that moment the relationship officially ended, so everything felt strange, it was as if two people were now just living in the same space.

The following morning think we both felt OK, we smiled, spoke a little, there was an atmosphere but not a negative one. I quickly left.

I am now single again, it's not ideal but I feel so much better and I'm actually getting my life back. Thank you, Aunty Bronwyn you've allowed me to take charge of my life and I feel so much better in every way. It often just takes that bit of a push to do something, and listening to you, pushed me. I even feel better in myself now because I understand my feelings better and not allow them to get the better of me. Thank you again. Leon.

Assumptions are the termites of relationships.

Henry Winkler

2

SINGLE MOTHER, WITH THE TEENAGE BOYS

Margery writes in. Aunty Bronwyn I'm a single mother of three teenage boys, I love them to bits, but to be honest they are more than a handful and are at times very disrespectful. I was just "going with the flow" doing my best, but things were progressively getting worse and me not having a life at all, almost a slave to my children I was just living on my wits.

A friend phoned me up and said to listen to your show, and I did. It was an awakening for me, in my mind it was literally about me. You were so right, I'm entitled to a life and respect regardless of who I am and the situation I'm in. The advice you gave was priceless, as you say, "throw the situation back on to-itself", so I did. I took your example to heart, churning word for word in my mind, I was so fuelled up because I was literally going down-hill health wise and mentally too. I said to the boys, the next time you misbehave I'm going to slap you, you can then phone social services or even the police and tell them what I have done. They will send someone around, you can tell them you don't like living here and that I'm a bad person.

They police will arrange to place you somewhere else for your safety and where you can be happy. I will then have my freedom, I will no-longer be a slave, and I'll the house to myself and then we will all be happy. Deep down I was trembling but managed to keep my cool for a while. They laughed, called my bluff, so I slapped (not hard) my eldest son and I literally phoned social services as I was right in the mood – although I didn't connect as luckily it was out of hours. The look on their faces. I felt very mean deep down, and as their mother I felt terrible doing such things, but I felt liberated too.

Things changed almost instantly. The change was miraculous, I felt that the boys had realised they had crossed the line and now you wouldn't believe how wonderful they are (well, nearly). Thank you, Aunty Bronwyn life is so much better all-around and even the boys seem so much happier too. Very best wishes Margery.

> ***Teenagers only have to focus on themselves - its not until we get older that we realize that other people exist.***
>
> *Jennifer Lawrence*

3

AGGRESSIVE MANAGER AT WORK

Philip writes in. Aunty Bronwyn we have a very bombastic manageress at work, quite a big character and with the size to match, as well as a loud voice. I suspect she gets away with what she does because her manager and boss are very timid, so she seems to be their mouthpiece. The trouble is she almost bullies people by saying, you do this and you that, and you and you do this, which goes way beyond duty and work. She's getting carried away now and life is not that pleasant for any of us particularly my assistant who I learned she is on tranquilisers.

One of the girls in the office heard your radio show and recommended me to listen in, I must admit I was very sceptical but listened to your topic on Taking Ownership. I was fixed to your every word when you said, "turn the problem around and fire it back at them". I just knew what I had to do, I just needed to hear you Aunty Bronwyn and that gave me the courage to light the fuse to what I needed to do.

With your further programme advice in mind, I wrote a letter to the MD and copied many others, all of whom agreed to what I had to say. Complaining of weak management, bullying, being victims and harassment, the usual works, but it was in effect all true. I mentioned that all those copied knew of the content and supported the letter, and I didn't send it to personnel because I didn't want it to be watered down of trivialised either.

I think the Director who received the letter was really taken back as he didn't quite know what to say when I called to see him. Far from being nervous, I was ready for a fight, and prepared to go to the press and civil courts and everything else. As it happened he was genuinely concerned and knew the manageress was a bit of a battle axe but not to this extent and things would change that morning, which they did. It's amazing that a few choice words in the right place can change everything. Thank you so much Aunty Bronwyn Philip.

A problem well stated is a problem half-solved.

Charles Kettering

4

DOMINEERING RELIGIOUS FAMILY

Taric writes. Aunty Bronwyn. He says I come from a very staunch Muslim family. Its' true, unconditional love doesn't exist in many Islamic families just rules and if you break them you get beaten or shouted at. Everyone lives a robotic life and hides behind a façade, everything is pretend or show for the family. Is there anything so stupid and pathetic?

For years I've been living a double life, one when out with friends – non -Muslim ones, and one life when I'm at home. One evening at a friend's I heard your show on "taking ownership or taking charge of your life". I just felt a shiver down my spine, I knew that you were talking to me, I suddenly became very angry and at the same time felt lightened by it all. I thought my home life is barbaric and pathetic I deserve better than this. I made plans for my own flat, moved out my things slowly and then just left. No forwarding address nothing. The best move I have made in my life, ever.

I waited for the pathetic phone calls from family members to start such as "your mother is dying, your father is ill, the family miss you", which predictably arrived, etc. What a pack of lies, they wouldn't know the truth if it hit them. It's possibly not the right way to go about things, but you know Aunty Bronwyn, I have a life and I'm really enjoying it away from this religious fantasyland where I lived before. Thank you so much, your advice has literally given me a life I never knew existed and a life with meaning too.

Everything smells better and looks better now I'm away from that toxic dysfunctional environment. Thank you once again Aunty Bronwyn.... Taric.

5

MIXED RACE / MULTI-CULTURAL MARRIAGE

We have a letter here from a couple Cheneil and Joseph who say. Aunty Bronwyn, we are what is termed a "multi-racial couple", that is black and white to be blunt. We have been going out with each other for a number of years and intend to get married very shortly. Together we have developed new common friends and have lots of interests and in fact we already have a "life" together.

Our respective families know of us but only just begrudgingly tolerate the situation, I'm sure dreading that day when they were to learn that we wanted to get married. Well, Aunty Bronwyn that day arrived. The "bombshell" of marriage comes into the conversation and it's like world war three and four rolled into one and possibly bit more. The stuff supposedly loving parents come out with, that gross selfishness of them, nothing to do with us just them, and although we expected some of it, it was however quite vociferous in content.

We were at a friend's house one evening shortly after relaying the "dreaded night's" events and they said listen to this, "The Aunty Bronwyn Show", we were chilling out with a glass of wine discussing the negativity of our parents trying to find a resolution. We listened, the room was completely silent as you spoke of "taking charge of your life". It is just so simple. What you said and what you suggested couldn't have been better placed and opportune. It's down to love nothing more. Our life is ours, we are the only ones to live it. We are not owned by anyone else, it was just so enlightening and freeing.

Our decision had been cemented that night, we are being married with or without parents or indeed anyone who doesn't want to come. We are marrying each other not our respective parents. Yes, it would be disappointing if they didn't come but the rest of our lives isn't going to be run by their selfish loveless stupidity and negativity, and disregard for our happiness, and that's final. Aunty Bronwyn a big thank you from both of us for your advice and an invite is in the post for you. God bless you.

You don't choose your family. They are God's gift to you, as you are to them.

Desmond Tutu

6

UNIVERSITY STUDENT, GOING HER OWN WAY AGAINST THE FAMILY

We have a letter here from Sandra, a student who is finishing university this year, who says. Aunty Bronwyn for some time now I've been uneasy about how my life is going. Academically I'm quite good in that I find learning easy as some of my friends have to slog hard all the time just to keep up. My parents have been supportive, but I realised that their support has in many cases been because I'm doing what they wanted me to do for their kudos, over and above a good education – for which I am very grateful.

I've come to that time in my life where values change, and my ideas are mine and not the product or desires of others including my parents. I have had a bit of a conflict within for some time in trying to assimilate this and find a way forward. My university girlfriend who is in a similar situation called me one evening all excitedly saying that she had made a decision to tell her parents what she was going to do, leave the university and get a vocational course which was her to a T. I couldn't help but hear a change in her voice and attitude. She told me she had listened to your show on 'Taking Charge of your life' and it all fell into place.

So, I listened to it and it had the same effect in that I immediately knew what I wanted to do. No hysteria, no bad words or shouting matches, no confrontation, after all my life isn't subject to anyone else's negotiation, as you quite rightly mentioned. You also stated "love" being the groundwork of life.

I told my parents, not a very good reception to say the least. I half expected that and was a bit disappointed and hurt, but nevertheless I have to live my life. I now have a part time job, I don't receive any money from them, I live as I want, I'm really happy and I'm in talks with a number of companies as to potentially good jobs. But you know Aunty Bronwyn I'm me and I just love it. Thank you so much. My parents will get over it all, just give it time, but meanwhile – life is on my terms. Thank you once again Aunty Bronwyn, love Sandra....

Vision is the art of seeing what is invisible to others.

Jonathan Swift

7

INCEST / RAPE IN RELIGIOUS FAMILY

We have a letter here from Fizal who says. Aunty Bronwyn I was quite a staunch Muslim scholar and wouldn't hear anything at all against Islam and overlooked all the evil things that are happening in the Islamic world – they just didn't register with me. I then found out that my sister had been abused by my father and my mother knew, but like all good Muslim families bad stuff happens and nobody talks about it.

My sister came to me in a desperate almost suicidal situation not knowing what to do. I just flipped inside all the rubbish I had been fed suddenly confronted me, my whole family living an ongoing lie. I had to tell a friend of mine just to get it all off my chest and he was for telling the police there and then, but I persuaded him not to as we had nowhere to go and the home would be an even worse place. So, he suggested we both live with him and his wife as they had an annex on their house until we sorted things out. His wife said to listen to your Show one evening on Taking Ownership and 'throwing back the problem on to those who caused it'.

This was new to me I would have never listened to your programmes before. Wow, my sister and I were in tears, having been fed a diet of propaganda all our lives and now we can be as we want to be.

We moved in to my friend's, we informed the police, who were actually great, it was all very traumatic, but we are so pleased that we made the break. It can't put back my sister's ordeal, but she is now free, happy and smiles and laughs which she hasn't done for such a long time. All I'm going to say from someone for whom all this is very new is thank you Aunty Bronwyn, you've given us the power back to run our lives we both can't thank you enough. Best Fizal.

> *I love you when you bow in your mosque, kneel in your temple, pray in your church. For you and I are sons of one religion, and it is the spirit.*
>
> *Khalil Gibran*

8

CITY TYCOON HAS HEALTH SHOCK AND MID LIFE CAREER CHANGE

Francis has written to us and says. Aunty Bronwyn I never ever thought I'd be writing to someone like you. I am a reasonably wealthy trader on the stock market and have accumulated my wealth over the years. I have lived an extravagant and egocentric life style because I could. This style of life can take a hold of you more than you know, you live in a bubble, literally, where outside circumstances aren't important, and neither are other people, they are just "anybodys"…

I was then diagnosed with a serious medical condition that literally meant stop what you are doing now or there may not be a tomorrow, this after seeing top specialists in the UK, USA and Germany. It was like pulling the plug on life, my ego was just shattered and without that being fuelled life wasn't worth living – so I thought. My secretary who is a brilliant lady told me to listen to your show on 'taking ownership' on life. I though "what on earth can this radio Aunty Bronwyn tell me?" however, I was feeling so low I thought "what the hell" do it. I not only listened to that but many of your other Shows too.

It was like being back to school, everything I had treasured of recent date fell away, and I actually saw another life developing that was real and wholesome. It didn't happen overnight, but I developed another life strategy and all my inner qualities, likes, dislikes, aptitudes now started to be put into perspective or shine, and I really felt a purpose something that was missing previously from my life.

I now run a small business now which I love, little stress but great fun and the few employees are great and love it too. I'm now contented, and I mix with many other people and share a camaraderie which I haven't done for years. There is a life after all for all of us, that I think anyone can enjoy if you allow it to happen, I even do voluntary work which is so enormously satisfying. Aunty Bronwyn you are worth a million dollars, no, even ten million dollars wearing my trading hat, thank you very much for your Shows. I've even recommended them to my previous colleagues too. Best wishes Francis.

He who has health, has hope; and he who has hope, has everything.

Thomas Carlyle

9

MARRIED WOMAN FINDS LESBIAN PARTNER

I have a letter here from Natasha who says. Aunty Bronwyn it is weird writing to you, but I heard by accident your programme on taking ownership and I just thought, right, I have to do this now whilst I have time or before it is too late.

I'm a middle aged plus married woman with two grown up children. The relationship between my husband and myself is and has been platonic now for quite some time. We get on well but go on our own separate paths. Some time ago I met and fell in love with another woman, it just happened, we have been seeing each other for some time now but it was when convenient more than on a regular basis. I think my husband thought I was having an affair, but it suited him, so he had his freedom also. Not the most satisfactory situation but like many things it works for a while. After hearing your programme on Taking Control I told my husband of the affair who was a little shocked but took it all in good form.

I'm now living with my girlfriend who is also my age, and we are enjoying this companionship enormously. My family know, and they have accepted it, in fact in coming out to them so did my son who I had no idea he was gay either, which was a big shock to me. However, I'm just happy that he is happy, because without happiness in life what is there left?

Possibly this is a weird family situation, but you are so right Aunty Bronwyn. We all have to live our lives we can't live them for others nor demand others live the way we want them to.

I'm so pleased I stumbled upon your show and would just like to say a big, big thank you for allowing me to bring happiness back into my life and seeing it from a better perspective. Thank you, Aunty Bronwyn hugs Natasha.

> ***Falling in love and having a relationship are two different things.***
>
> **Keanu Reeves**

10

GAY ASIAN BOY STANDS HIS GROUND

Sunil writes. Aunty Bronwyn I'm a gay Asian guy, I've always been gay, and my parents found out at an early age. It was a bit of a shock initially, but my mother didn't want me to move away so over time they got used to it all. I've never really had any problems with it because it's me and I feel comfortable with it. My parents initially had problems with the family and all that "cultural stuff" that Asian families hold on to then wonder why things never go smoothly. But I never cared about that and giving them their due my parents have always supported me as have my two eldest sisters and younger brother also.

I have been going out with my boyfriend Anil now for over two years and we have been on holiday together a number of times and attend family functions which is always amusing to say the least, it definitely gets people talking. Having said that my grandmother is my number one fan, she's fabulous so if anyone in the family say anything bad she's on to them straight away, it's a bit like The Kumars. (British Asian Family comedy show).

I'm just writing to say Aunty Bronwyn your programme on "Taking Ownership" I got my parents, my sisters, my brother and my grandmother to listen to and since then we have all been "ultra- cool" about various aspects of our lives, because provided there is love involved then harmony should be a norm, nothing less. I got Anil to listen to it and his parents too. And because my parents accept me they feel more comfortable with him, amazing really. Just a big big thank you for your Show everyone should listen to it.

Thank you, Aunty Bronwyn, big hugs Sunil...

Parents are the ultimate role models for children. Every word, movement and action has an effect. No other person or outside force has a greater influence on a child than the parent.

*** Bob Keeshan***

11

ITALIAN SHUNNED BY JEALOUS PARENTS OVER DAUGHTER'S DEATH

I have a letter here from Alfredo who says. Aunty Bronwyn, I had been going out with a lovely English girl Sue for quite some time, I'm Italian. My mother became ill, so I went for a brief visit to see her in Naples. Sue's parents never really liked me or were very cold as if I wasn't good enough. Sue told me not to take any notice as it was jealousy as I actually come from a very well to do family.

During my visit to Italy Sue became very ill and died very quickly of severe complications. I thought it strange that I hadn't heard but I had also to deal with my elderly mother and facilities she needed. None of my calls to Sue's mobile or the family home were returned. When I came back to the UK I had to go around to the family home to see why there was no response and was met with an almost aggressive reception and the terrible news. Not even invited in, I just turned away and went home in a daze. I contacted some of our mutual friends who were very supportive and came with me to the funeral. I was devastated, worn out, lost, so fragile I could hardly think. It was just as if someone had pulled the plug on my life, coupled with the fact both of my parents had ailing health too.

I was at a friend's house and I heard your programme on bereavement. I just thought at last I have someone who knows what I'm going through and put it into a real perspective. Death is all about how you feel, no one else. If, the deceased loved you then they would have failed in life (and death) not wishing what life you have left is not a happy one.

What others think is not your business. Life is for the living and the lovely memories of those you shared with the deceased.

It is still going to take time to get over Sue's loss for me she was everything I could have wanted. But your words on life, love, death and purpose rejuvenated my inner self and has comforted me such a lot. I keep listening to your broadcast. Thank you, Aunty Bronwyn...

Death is not the greatest loss in life. The greatest loss is what dies inside us while we live.

Norman Cousins

12

YOUNG GAY LOVER COPES WITH ELDER PARTNERS DEATH

We have a letter from Martyn. He says. Aunty Bronwyn, I was late in "coming out" in my life having had a succession of miserable relationships in the past, which was probably down to me supressing my real feelings. I met by chance a guy quite a bit older than myself and we just clicked. For the first time in my life I felt really happy and emotionally secure and loved. I just felt complete and full of fun and meaning and all the things you want to feel.

This however didn't last long. I'm in my late twenties he was 43. He was fit, went to the gym always full of beans, never ill then suffered a massive heart attack. Evidently, he had a heart defect that had not been picked up previously. My world stopped, I was in disbelief, life was at last for me just taking off and then nothing. To say I was devastated doesn't come into it. His family were excellent and supportive as were mine, but it still doesn't change anything. I just couldn't get out of my mind what had happened and just when I had experienced what life should be like it all came tumbling down.

A friend of mine told me of you and that I should listen to your show on bereavement. I did, and I have to say it made the world of difference it has encapsulated all we had together and brought meaning, love, life and what we shared. It hasn't been lost it was wonderful. It takes time to get over the loss, but emotionally about life I feel so much better now and can continue. The love, the time we shared will never be lost, the experience we both had together is still priceless. You are right too that life is for the living and I know he would definitely want me to be happy at any cost because he was so full of beans and laughter himself.

Thank you so much Aunty Bronwyn big hugs Martyn.

> *I would rather die a meaningful death than to live a meaningless life.*
>
> *Corazon Aquino*

13

ELDERLY WIDOW COMES TO TERMS WITH FRIENDS WHO SHOW UP ON DEATH OF HUSBAND ONLY.

We have received a letter from Agnes who says. Aunty Bronwyn. My husband and I have been married nearly 40 years. Like anyone we have had our ups and downs, but you just get on with it. If a relationship is good, it's worth saving. My husband was quite well known and liked and had a lot of friends. Over the past year he unfortunately became quite ill and was either in hospital or in bed at home.

When he died my children were very good and arranged everything, it went so well, I had to do very little. At the service the church was packed, I was quite taken back and people who I never knew came up saying they had known George for 30 years or more. I was a little disconcerted afterwards that why did so many people turn up to see my husband when he was dead and couldn't be bothered when he was alive?

My daughter was visiting me and started talking about a show she had listened to and suggested that I might like to listen to it. I thought it would possibly make good listening too, so I tuned in. I happened to just by chance hear your show on bereavement. It was excellent, it made so much sense and really made me feel at ease with my recent situation and about all those who just show up when it is all too late.

It also put into perspective my views on what I thought should have been and weren't, realising that I don't control others only myself, and divorcing myself at that moment from me trying to make sense of everything suddenly lifted a great burden that made everything become clear. The result of this put my mind at peace and I viewed everything just for what it was, the important thing was I was there, and it was a great day which went well with my family around me. Thank you, Aunty Bronwyn, I told my daughter and my sons to listen to that Show as I really think it helps put your mind at ease. Thanks again Agnes.

The timing of death, like the ending of a story, gives a changed meaning to what preceded it.

Mary Catherine Bateson

14

OVERCOMING DIFFICULT FAMILY RELATIONSHIPS

Claire has written to us and says. Aunty Bronwyn. Our family is one of those that is always at loggerheads with each other. If there is something to fall out about or take the wrong way, then we are the number one family. Extended periods of not talking are all par for the course as is my mother having always to be right.

Recently one of my sisters died of an illness and of course we all were to meet at the funeral. You would have thought this would have brought us all together, but no, it was just another reason to have a go at each other and our mother to complain and be angry at everyone for any reason that came into her mind. My nieces and nephews are but strangers as we rarely meet and common friends of the family gave up ages ago.

A week before the funeral I happen to hear your show on bereavement, love, life, people, situations, death, the aftermath. I was so taken back in what you had to say, it was our dysfunctional family in every respect. But what was more telling being what you said about it all and its meaning and purpose. Where is the love, and that is what the whole problem has been with our family, everything was selfishly based upon conditional love and not real love?

After your show I was so elevated as I now understood everything. The funeral came it was very good – as funerals go, I smiled at everyone, said hello to my brothers and sisters, complemented my mother and took all her abuse, then said it was lovely to have seen her and how nice she looked, which phased her no end. It was a fitting day to say farewell to my sister.

Since the funeral my parents and my brothers and sisters have phoned me, quite out of character but despite the odd remark they were quite civil and nice. Aunty Bronwyn you are just so right. Life is too short. Love is the answer anything less is just that, less. You also put into perspective bereavement which makes such a difference as all I can think of now is my lovely departed sister nothing else. Thank you Aunty Bronwyn I'm going to get all my relatives to listen to your show.

I don't think there's ever a winner in a feud. It's about emotional pain and an inability to conquer the pain.

Ryan Murphy

15

LONER AND SWAT LOSES BEST FRIEND IN SUICIDE

Helen writes. Aunty Bronwyn I have always been a bit of a swat at school and made good grades. I suppose I was always the loner and the odd one out too. I got into university. Whilst there I met someone just like myself Sarah, she was almost an identical copy of me and we just clicked. I think it is the first time in my life I've ever had a friend and someone who I could call anytime and trust to talk to, I'm sure she felt exactly the same about me too.

My family were very supportive of me, hers weren't supportive of her at all and if anything wanted her to work to bring money in, which would have been a big mistake because she was so clever and wanted to go into research. She had to fight to keep at university and was forever short of money which I helped her out at times even on my miserable grant. I was woken up very early one morning by the police to say that Sarah had died from an overdose and that I was possibly the only one who could give them some information about her. I was just devastated, I just went to pieces I was really in shock about it all, thinking it was a bad dream. The police were very helpful, and the police woman stayed with me until I got over the initial shock. The university were also very helpful in fact even those who I didn't know so well were so supportive, I can't thank them enough.

What I couldn't get over was why, when Sarah had everything to live for, this thought just plagued me constantly and I couldn't just get it out of my head. One evening a friend said had I listened to Aunty Bronwyn and I said I'm not into agony aunts, but she said this is different, so I listened to your show on bereavement, and it was different. It made such a difference to my thinking and my thought process and put into perspective love and death and friendship and life and everything else.

It takes time to get over missing a friend like her, but at least I feel more equipped to join life again and be a part of the bigger picture and not a recluse. I would just like to say thank you Aunty Bronwyn, you have made such a difference to my life as it is now, and I can now move onwards. Thank you again. Helen.

Suicide is a permanent solution to a temporary problem.

Phil Donahue

16

A DEAR AUNT DIES LEAVING DISTRAUGHT NIECE

Pippa writes in to say. Aunty Bronwyn an aunt of mine died some time ago suddenly, we were very close, and she was one of my few remaining relatives. She brought me up when I was young because of circumstances. I know we all have to go and can't choose when, but it left me really "high and dry" emotionally and I just couldn't get to grips with her having died and not being there.

By chance, I heard your broadcast-on Bereavement and it made such a difference, I cried with relief and understanding and really do understand now that life is about love, nothing more, everything else is how we exist.

I'm as close to my aunt now as ever and feel such inner peace. Thank you, Aunty Bronwyn you have brought such tranquillity to my life and restored my inner self which was very low. Kind wishes Pippa.

***Grief is in two parts.
The first is loss.
The second is the remaking of life.***

Anne Roiphe

17

COMING TO TERMS WITH WIFE'S DEATH

George writes to say. Aunty Bronwyn my wife died two years ago, she was terminally ill and we both knew the score. We had had a very happy life together and we spoke at length about that eventual day. We said everything we could say, although it's never enough, nevertheless we said what we wanted to and then that "eventual" day arrived.

It was still a devastating blow even though I was expecting it. That was two years ago, and I still couldn't get to grips with certain aspects of life and God and anything else that should be there. Then I heard your broadcast-on Bereavement. I'll say one thing you don't mince your words, but what you did say was just so real and warm and understanding and full of the reality of what life and death is all about.

Bereavement is something religions mess up completely or sound so sanctimonious and pompous and pathetic in their explanation. I felt so warm and close to my wife after your broadcast I was at last feeling a degree of peace and wasn't restless anymore. I still miss her terribly, but I also have a degree of closure that my life still has purpose and meaning and love that I need to uphold who I am for my wife now. Maybe I just can't explain it all any better, but I'd just like to say thank you so much you have no idea what that short broadcast did, it's opened up my life again. Thank you, Aunty Bronwyn.

18

FINDING HAPPINESS AGAIN AFTER MOTHER DIES

Aunty Bronwyn, Ayesha writes. Aunty Bronwyn. A number of years ago my younger brother died whilst on holiday in Pakistan. I'm not totally sure that it was all what it was said to be but with Muslim families nothing ever is.

Recently my mother died very suddenly. She was diagnosed with a condition and then just as quickly died. She was a lovely woman and stood up for me and my two brothers and always wanted us to do what we wanted to do and not follow what others wanted, which is what she had had to do. I feel so lost without her as she was almost my best friend too and I could say anything to her and even if I knew she wasn't too happy she would just smile at me and never judge, even my friends loved talking to her. I thought I'd get over it all by now or at least see life differently, but I so miss her.

Then I heard your broadcast-on bereavement and it made such a difference. Women in Islam are basically second-class citizens, and many behave like that, but I can hear my mum saying, don't believe it, there's nothing second class about you. When you spoke of death and love it all brought such a warm glow I could almost hear my mother saying what you said, it was wonderful. I feel so much better and I understand much better too and feel so close to my mother that I can go on now with a cheerful smile.

Thank you so much Aunty Bronwyn, I'm telling my friends about your broadcasts they should be made compulsory.

19

TWIN EVENTUALLY GETS OVER HIS BROTHER'S NEEDLESS DEATH

We have a letter here from Joe and he writes. Aunty Bronwyn I lost my twin brother Simon over a year ago now to a drink drive idiot who ran into him, he according to the paramedics died instantly. We did everything together, we were inseparable and now I feel there is such a void, I feel lost, I lack interest I just couldn't pull myself together. I kept expecting to see him or hear him in his bedroom but of course there's nothing, he's not there.

I was with a few friends at a friend's house one evening and she suggested that we listen to your show as she was a devoted fan of yours. We agreed as we knew she wanted to listen to you. The show was on bereavement. It's what I needed to hear because no matter what anyone says, when someone significant in your life goes it really hurts. You spoke of love, life, death and having your own individual purpose and I just couldn't have agreed more with it all.

You mentioned about those left behind and that life is for the living and the love which never dies between those who have died and those still living namely ourselves. I just started crying to myself as I could see Simon playing his tricks on me – as he did often, he was such fun, it was all so real, but I could also hear him saying what you had said and for that it all became so clear. When I went home I told my parents of the show and told them to listen to it, my mum was so overcome because she was still having problems of his needless death. Just to say thank you Aunty Bronwyn, you now have another devoted fan, thank you....

20

BROTHER AND SISTER LOSE PARENTS BUT BUILD LIFE AGAIN

Sue and Richard write to us and say. Aunty Bronwyn, nearly a year ago now we lost our parents when they went on holiday. We were doing our finals – my brother and myself – so we told them to go as we would just be swatting anyway. They went as it was a chance they had to enjoy a really good holiday and we would have the place to ourselves also. That feeling of "having the house to ourselves" soon dissipated in two days as both our parents were killed in an accident.

It's amazing how life can dramatically change within seconds. Suddenly we would never see them again, never say all those things you would have liked to, never say sorry or thank you, nothing. Then clearing their things out, it was a nightmare for both of us. I don't know what I would have done without my brother.

A girlfriend of mine came around one evening and we were just chatting, she suddenly mentioned about your shows and "why not give it a go", so I thought OK. Armed with two cups of tea we listened, and it happened by chance to be on bereavement. I just wish my brother had been in. Your show was amazing, it made me cry but it was a good cry, even my friend was crying. I can't tell you how much better I feel about life, death, my parents, my choices, love, my future. You covered it all in such a short space of time, direct and to the point but never the less it was with such a caring attitude that I warmed to everything you said.

When my brother came in I had to get him to download the show to listen to it, which he did, and I listened to it again with him. It made a difference to Richard, who unlike me bottles things up inside, but I could see that it had affected him deeply in a positive way. We stayed up late that night talking things over which we just couldn't have done before. Thank you so much Aunty Bronwyn, you have made such a difference to our lives, this should be more available for everyone who has suffered a bereavement to hear. Thank you again, big hug, Sue and Richard....

The greatest legacy one can pass on to one's children and grandchildren is not money or other material things accumulated in one's life, but rather a legacy of character and faith.

Billy Graham

21

GETTING A RELATIONSHIP BACK ON TRACK

Tim writes to us. Aunty Bronwyn, it's strange, after a period of time how relationships develop. My partner and I work hard and play hard, but I have to say she is the one who "wears the trousers" in the home. I'm happy or was happy just to go with it as I'm quite an easy-going person.

There comes a point however where that no longer is true, and one needs to do and get things into perspective as by default it gets too stilted one way and then everything starts to get unbalanced and not so nice. A strange thing happened, both of us listened to your Show on Taking Ownership together and I noticed it hit a nerve, and I knew that this was the moment I had to broach the situation from my perspective. Because you had laid the foundations already, what I had to say thereafter wasn't that difficult.

I confronted my partner calmly and said, "hear me out" and far from being a confrontational situation it was quite the opposite, it was just so marvellous. What you suggested wasn't difficult because it was honest and sincere. Thank you, Aunty Bronwyn for your advice, it's made such a difference with more openness to our relationship.

22

BREAKING THAT CULTURAL BUBBLE

I have a letter from Priti who writes. Aunty Bronwyn, my mother had an arranged marriage. She was very clever and beautiful when younger but was never allowed to develop any of her faculties and was confined to basically a worthless marriage. Life hasn't been easy, and my father is very moody and temperamental wanting his own way all the time. If it wasn't for the fact that he inherited some money I feel sure my mother would have left a long time ago and taken me and my brother with her. My eldest brother has now left the house and hardly ever speaks to my father and then it erupts into something very bad, although my brother always wins the arguments. As it happens my brother has done very well indeed in business and offered a flat for my mother and me as long as I want to stay there in a very nice area.

My mother is still relatively young and longs to meet other people in the community as she rarely was allowed to go out other than just shopping. I heard your programme on Taking Ownership and called my brother immediately, saying come and persuade our mother to go to this flat. Long story short, we have just moved, it's amazing I've never seen my mother so bubbly and happy and I'm so thrilled not to have my father moaning in the background and being judgemental. We both feel free at last and it has made so much difference.

Aunty Bronwyn your few words of wisdom just resonated so much that it swayed my thoughts and I then swayed my mother's thoughts to moving, both of us taking ownership of our lives. It's just great. Thank you so much again Aunty Bronwyn.

23

HOW AN ORTHODOX JEW FINDS REAL LOVE BY LEAVING HOME

Aunty Bronwyn I have a letter from Yaron who says. Aunty Bronwyn I come from a family of 4 boys and two girls of Orthodox Jews. Life hasn't been bad and as children we have been supported and cared for well, but it was a strict household and it therefore had its limitations, or it did for me, I always wanted what I couldn't have.

Anyway, I've fallen for this wonderful Christian girl and my intent is to get married to her. I say intend, I didn't know what to do until I heard your show at her house on Taking Ownership. Eventually when I told my family there were eruptions and fireworks and incriminations, and you name it, but that's par for the course and part of the dull boring hysteria show that orthodox families put on when they think they are losing or not getting their own way. (Where is the love now)?

It's all emotional blackmail stuff – it's inherent in their make-up it comes almost naturally, etc. But armed with this knowledge based upon what you said about taking ownership of your life, I did it, lived through it and stayed with a friend to keep the incessant wailing off the agenda. My girlfriend's family are lovely people and cool with it all and they like me and make me very welcome. The wedding will go ahead and one of my brothers has said he will attend so far.

But you are so right Aunty Bronwyn I have to live my life, live with the woman I love and not be dictated to or live a lie just to please selfish others that's not wholesome, it's all wrong.

It's not been easy, but your words on Taking Ownership just sounded so true and honest and right and I want to be with my future wife she means everything to me. So, thank you again Aunty Bronwyn, you're my shining star.

> ***Happy is the man who finds a true friend, and far happier is he who finds that true friend in his wife.***
>
> *Franz Schubert*

24

INDIAN GIRL REFUSES TO BE MARRIED OFF BY PARENTS

Pravine writes to us. Aunty Bronwyn. I come from a quite wealthy Indian family, or so I thought until one day I heard my parents talking to someone in the kitchen about me (I have another sister married and a younger brother).

The gist of the conversation was that if I married this person's son my father would get a lot of financial support for his company and a number of perks that go with it. I can't tell you how horrified I was to hear this. I was in two minds to barge in and state my case, because I'm quite like that but decided against it. I'm not a commodity for anyone and that's that. Yet I still didn't know what to do or how to get out of this as I knew there would be massive repercussions. I'm not a business transaction for anyone either.

I went to see a girlfriend of mine and just told her everything, I was in such a state. That evening she said have you ever listened to Aunty Bronwyn and I hadn't even heard of your shows, she said let's listen there may be some advice. It happened to be your show on taking charge or ownership, it couldn't have been a better subject. We both loved everything you said as it really placed my thoughts where I thought they should be. Now I was so fired up I can't tell you. I was just waiting for that moment when they would subtly drop the bombshell to me.

It happened a few days later and I don't think they knew what had hit them, I told my father I don't care if he goes bust and lives in a tent that's his business but I'm not part of it, I was almost ready to start throwing things. I left and stayed at my friend's house and turned off my phone that night. Fortunately, it's all – well almost, back to normal, wedding thoughts off the agenda and anything else off too.

But without your pep talk on the radio Aunty Bronwyn it would have been an ordeal that I would have struggled with. But as you said, "turn it back towards the problem" and don't accept it at all, and above all value your own life, because it's your life, no one else's. It worked a treat. Thank you so much Aunty Bronwyn.

> *You're either part of the solution or you're part of the problem.*
>
> *Eldridge Cleaver*

25

GETTING A LIFE AGAIN AFTER HUSBANDS AFFAIR

Simone has written to us and says. Aunty Bronwyn I found out my husband was having an affair. It was one of those little things that gave it away and you just know your partner and what they say and how they say it or at times what they don't say.

The person was in fact a woman who was introduced to us who had separated from her husband recently and wanted some "time" to get over it. Evidently, she wanted more than just time and the affair started. It was a shock to find out as all your hopes and trust just fall apart right in front of you, a picture of nothingness is there, and you feel so empty, lonely and cold inside and drained and used and discarded. I lived with these feelings for a few days not telling anyone wondering what to do.

It just happened that my brother popped around with his children to give me my birthday present. I burst into tears as I couldn't hold it all in any longer. After he left his wife phoned me later who I get along with very well and we had a long chat. She then had to see to the children but said listen to Aunty Bronwyn and told me where to tune in or download the show. The show happened to be on "taking ownership or taking charge of your life" and I must admit listening to it gave me a lot of confidence and support as I knew what I had to do.

My feelings I had to deal with, but the fact that what you said made me respect who I am and not give in to the "poor old me" syndrome helped enormously. The strategy you advised helped clarify in my mind what was to come and what I needed to do, I just kept thinking of your words and it makes me feel so much better in every way. Thank you, Aunty Bronwyn, you really have made such a difference in a difficult situation.

> *If we listened to our intellect, we'd never have a love affair. We'd never have a friendship. We'd never go into business, because we'd be cynical. Well, that's nonsense. You've got to jump off cliffs all the time and build your wings on the way down.*
>
> *Ray Bradbury*

26

INCEST – LOVE OR SEX? (1)
BROTHER AND SISTER IN A RELATIONSHIP

A letter arrived from Samantha who has said she is concerned because of her secret. I have been having relations with my brother for a number of years now we are both very happy with it. My brother is one year older than I am. It started in our late teens we were from dysfunctional parents and our mutual comforting and support lead eventually to sex.

We know the legality and we don't plan on having children, especially as we may carry our parent's gene's which would be disastrous for them. I have been listening to your shows for some time now and I was amazed that your topic one evening was on Incest as you had had letters similar to mine. It's a subject rarely spoken about and it is so judged, in fact the aspect of love within it rarely ever gets taken into consideration.

I listened to your comments about life and love and repercussions of our actions and agreed with every word. I also brought to mind your on-going comments that your life is your life and no one else's ever, provided you didn't harm others. I discussed it all with my brother. Incest I know to many is not a very palatable thing, but we are both so happy and together are survivors of the past. Whilst I may never disclose "my secret" I really do feel so much better for your humane and sensible comments, it has made a great difference to how we both feel and interact with life in general. I also know that society is one thing, people are another and life is something different yet again, full of variables as nothing is "etched in stone" absolutely nothing. Thank you Aunty Bronwyn you have really made such a difference to our lives. Thank you. Samantha.

> *Three can keep a secret,*
> *if two of them are dead.*
>
> *Benjamin Franklin*

27

INCEST – LOVE OR SEX? (2)
BROTHERS IN A RELATIONSHIP

Within the mounds of letters, we get on the same subject we have a letter from Jason who writes. Aunty Bronwyn I heard your show on Incest a while ago and it really did ring a chord within me. Only your programme would talk about something like that and not make it a glorified issue. Since early teens I have been having sex with my brother. Like many pubescent teens you start fooling around but for us it was more than that we were always together and rarely except at school apart from each other.

We were as one even to dressing in almost the same type of clothes. Our parents I think had a vague inkling that we were exceptionally close, but as we didn't do drugs or drank little they were I think just pleased that they didn't have all that to worry about. Away from each other it actually hurt, we just kept thinking about each other constantly and looking forward to meeting up later on. Just seeing my brother walking towards me makes me feel really warm and tingly and happy. My brother won a scholarship and had to move, it was devastating I can't tell you, like something drastically missing in your life. I eventually left home and moved in with him.

It's very difficult even in gay circles living together and although we are accepted as brothers sharing we don't have boyfriends or flings with others like our friends do and that needs some careful explaining just not to arouse suspicion.

AGONY LETTERS

It's not that we are ashamed or embarrassed far from it but it's just this stereotype idea of "incest" and that it is something dark and degenerate and about bad people who indulge in such things and are really subnormal.

Our secret may or may not come out in time, however after listening to what you had to say my inner confidence has grown enormously and I relayed that to my brother who I know was enlightened by it as it seemed to affect him thought wise more than it did me. Your open views on life and love certainly hit home, they were spot on and as for other's opinions as to your life and how you live it, it made me smile.

We are both early twenties and have a lot of time ahead of us including life itself, however after hearing what you said we are both far better prepared and far more stable in our reactions now than ever before. One of your shows on taking ownership said "turn situations back on themselves" don't accept other's responsibilities, ideas or comments when it's none of their business towards yourself. If they don't like it fine, but what's all that got to do with me, deal with it yourself.

Life changing Aunty Bronwyn, just life changing. Big hugz Jason and Elliot.

28

INCEST – LOVE OR SEX? (3)
SISTERS IN A RELATIONSHIP

Betsy and Tabatha have written. Aunty Bronwyn we are identical sisters, even our parents at times got confused between us which was very amusing as we would play tricks on them, although they have got used to it. Like all children you bath together sleep together play together, dress alike, share toys, all the usual children's stuff and in our case shared the same birthday too. There's three minutes difference between us.

Now thirty years on in our mid-thirties we are still together, enjoying life as it is and the ups and downs which there have been their fair share. Our parents know about us, it came as a shock but it's all in the past now. I think the biggest problem they faced is "what do we tell people". But I think they've come up with an answer, but as you say Aunty Bronwyn it's for them to come to terms with it all, this is not of our doing even by default. Also, we can't be an excuse to ourselves nor put ourselves down to make the scenario fit with what others think, we must always uphold who we are and that is our right.

Your Show a while ago on incest was very enlightening and put into place a number of aspects of who we are and our relationship. It also affirmed to us that we need to be accepted for who we are otherwise we are surrounding ourselves with the wrong people. As you say it's amazing that those who are unwholesome, liars, cheats and worse will criticize you just for the sake of it but they need a mirror to see who they are first, at least we do no harm to anyone else.

AGONY LETTERS

I know this is a taboo subject and governed by all kinds of legal stuff, but morally what is wrong with two people who are in love, no children involved just both parties doing their best for each other at their one chance to be happy in life. Anyway, Aunty Bronwyn, thank you so much for your thoughts and words of wisdom they really did make a great difference to us. We love your shows and are your number one fans...

> *My strength and my weakness are twins in the same womb.*
>
> *Marge Piercy*

29

INCEST – LOVE OR SEX? (4)
FATHER AND DAUGHTER

Aunty Bronwyn I'm writing to you because I heard your programme on Incest which is very rare and if there is a programme it's all full of weird psychologists and even more weird counsellors with deep involved opinions and it never ever touches why!!!

I'm going to really start the taboo cycle going because I've been living with my father for six years and I love every minute of it. We even have a child although the father is "unknown" as far as registration is concerned. I was never abused, lead on, never had a weird childhood, had boyfriends, just like everyone else really. My mother died and after the funeral my father wanted to move to the coast to a smaller home which he did. I stayed on and helped him move with my brother who lives quite a long way away and he visited father once a year. After my brother left I started cooking, cleaning, looking after the home and my father said I could stay as long as I liked as he enjoyed the company and the meals, which he joked about.

Something happened after a while we just got so close as friends enjoying each-others company and of course the unthinkable happened. But far from the repugnant thoughts that one could have brought to mind it was quite the opposite and for the first time I really enjoyed a relationship to the level that this gave. The rest now is history. I know all the ins and outs of having children, but our daughter is fine and healthy, and we are a loving family now.

My brother has no idea and I don't plan to tell him as I know he would be so upset. The point of writing Aunty Bronwyn is that your programme on incest was fabulous as you looked at the situation from a pragmatic none judgmental point of view as it really happens and not from a pre-judged 'technical' aspect which is inhuman and narrow. Thank you, Aunty Bronwyn the world needs more of you….

Time is too slow for those who wait, too swift for those who fear, too long for those who grieve, too short for those who rejoice, but for those who love, time is eternity.

Henry Van Dyke

30

INCEST – LOVE OR SEX? (5)
TWO SISTERS AND A MALE PARTNER

Aunty Bronwyn Pam writes in to say. I listened to your show on incest and I must say it was not only refreshing but you put into perspective such relationships which is far far beyond what other dull programmes have put forward on the same subject. Without judgment you have encapsulated those who are involved without treating them as objects to be criticised by a committee just to point a finger at just to make an interesting show.

I'm in a very strange relationship with my sister and her husband. When we were little my sister and I were very close and this lead to a teen relationship which lasted until I left for university. There I met a man who I had a relationship with for many years. Meanwhile my sister had found a man and got married, it was all very pleasant and we all got on well. My relationship eventually fell apart and I dated a few women, it just happened nothing was planned and no ulterior motive, it just happened.

Time went by and our parents passed away leaving the estate to my sister and myself. The clearing of the house brought us back together again and whilst we were clearing the house the affair started. I enquired about her husband who I got on with and she said he wouldn't mind at all. Well, we got together eventually at a certain time and had our threesome, it was just like clockwork, my initial nerves went, and we have all three lived together ever since, and not a moment's upset or jealousy nor anything else.

For those who can't or don't understand what has developed that's OK keep quiet. For those who do understand or find themselves in a strange experience, just be yourself. Aunty Bronwyn you keep saying don't take other's inabilities to heart or keep them on your mind if they can't understand, that's their lookout, don't try and fix or excuse yourself just to fit in with others.

Never ever reduce your value or put yourself down no matter who it is. What wonderful advice that is, keep your respect and understand that life isn't black and white, and you are entitled to be who you are as long as you don't hurt others. God bless you Aunty Bronwyn listening to you has enhanced our lives.... Thank you...

Life is really simple, but we insist on making it complicated.

Confucius

31

UNMARRIED AND UNWANTED PREGNANCY SECOND TIME AROUND

Samantha writes. Aunty Bronwyn I have two children both unplanned, I'm unmarried and don't have a partner. I'm living on State Benefits and apart from others in my position who empathise with me I get cold looks from everyone else, even my family are ashamed of me and can't get to grips with what I've done when it was totally preventable, and I could have had a better life than I have now.

I was so low last week as I had an argument (which developed over an incident) with another woman with two children who is married, and she had such a go at me and deep down I knew she was right. A friend told me about your Shows and I'm now a regular listener. One show in particular about "taking ownership" that was me to a T. Your response to those who had similar situations was like talking to me directly. As you said we can't change the past, we shouldn't even look there because we are not going that way, we should only look to the future and there we can change the whole of our lives.

I think this was the conversation that I was looking for as it made a real impact upon me and I hope at the same time I can make my children proud of me and themselves and not be embarrassed as being stupid mistakes by some thoughtless young person. I love my children even more now as their future is a number one priority and now I hardly ever see any of the other single mums as they seem to be in a "dull collective and not inspiring at all".

I know this isn't for everyone Aunty Bronwyn but your show on "Loneliness" last night also hit home and it's down to me to change that. Thank you for being that thoughtful friend who speaks her mind, one that makes total sense and doesn't judge. Thank you again Aunty Bronwyn – Sam.

Loneliness expresses the pain of being alone and solitude expresses the glory of being alone.

Paul Tillich

32

AFTER THE FAILED SUICIDE ATTEMPT

Neville writes in. Aunty Bronwyn a while ago now I attempted suicide, it didn't work, everything went wrong, even with that. My best friend found me in an unconscious state, he shouldn't have been home that night, but the weather cancelled his train journey. I'm over it now, I've had counselling and it's amazing the few friends I have are really supportive. I know what I did was not right and that there is always a way out, but sometimes your mind closes in on you and you see absolutely nothing but darkness and no hope whatsoever.

It's a terrible feeling, being totally alone with no solutions, no future, no way out, no hope, no one to turn to, just nothing in abundance. (Even though there are places you can contact). You just want to get out of that dark damp evil place for good, with no chance of ever having to return to it again. Life is for others to make a go out of, which they do, but for some reason you weren't dealt that card. For you, well nothing exists, and you can't even fathom ways of getting out of it, it's just science fiction so it's bye bye world, I've had enough of this I just can't take any more. END.

Whilst getting over my failed attempt I had a lot of time on my hands and I listened to your Shows. I was also reflective about what I had done and it's ironic that once you have told everyone why you attempted what you did solutions do become available. My best friend was in a bad state for a few days too and really angry with me, it was not very nice what I had put him through just for what I wanted in life. Listening to your shows which were often very funny made me laugh, which I hadn't done for some time, it was like piecing my life back together jigsaw style.

Every show had something that I could relate to, the emotional aspects you capture so well, and they mean so much to everyone. I now feel so much better I'm even seeing life differently and can see that my hope is so real too. It's no longer something abstract it's all within my grasp. It takes time to get over the ordeal of suicide – wanting to end your life, but as you say a positive mind closes the doors of the past and opens up a future and that is so true. You also need positive supportive people around you all the time and no longer will I ever listen to negative people they can go their own way.

I could go on but Aunty Bronwyn just the biggest thank you ever, you are a life line to those who get lost in life. I'll telling everyone to listen to you. Big big eternal hug Aunty Bronwyn love you Neville.

> ***We need to change the culture of this topic and make it OK to speak about mental health and suicide.***
> ***Luke Richardson***

33

WHEN YOU'VE FAILED ALL TOO OFTEN

Aunty Bronwyn Gareth writes to us. Aunty Bronwyn I come from a good family, have no complaints as such, had good family support both emotionally and financially so basically what am I complaining about? Over the many years I've tried a number of projects, all have been given the green light by friends and fellow businessmen in that their thinking was "these projects are really good and have potential".

For one reason or another none of them took off. If something could go wrong even at the last minute, it went wrong, and it was back to square one yet again. Treading water was becoming a way of life and at times the water level was almost reaching dangerous levels. I've always been positive in life and it really does make a difference to your outlook. However subliminally it all gets to you deep inside, the constant toll of trying, developing good ideas, and then it all going flat. The "here we go again" routine sounding all too familiar.

You kept saying things in your Shows like "It only takes a small pin to burst a big balloon" or "One match is all you need to start a raging fire" or "hope is the only opportunity you need". Also, things like scientists fail for years on end every day trying to discover a new drug or solution, but they do eventually succeed and often in the process discover something else of equal worth. You also keep saying that failure is successes best bed fellow for without one the other doesn't exist. Two other things you constantly say or talk about "love" and "never ever give up". Failure doesn't exist until you stop.

For you Aunty Bronwyn failure is just a word and then it is relative. Failure for most people is something grossly negative and shameful or full of regret. In listening to your Shows this overwhelming positivity suddenly got a hold of me within and I thought OK, I'm not giving up and went away with my current project. It wasn't plain sailing I have to admit and at times I often had second thoughts as to who am I kidding myself, but I then thought "Never, ever give up" and then I thought to myself "sod it I'm not giving up" and I didn't.

When success eventually hits you, you wonder what it is, you can't believe that it's happening and that it is not a flash in the pan, it's the real deal. Aunty Bronwyn I just have to say thank you, for when I was low and feeling so dejected you came along and basically said "so what" keep trekking. I did, and I am so glad, it has made as you said everything just so worthwhile. Thank you, Aunty Bronwyn you are a real guiding or shining star or maybe both... Thank you so much. Gareth.

> *Emancipate yourselves from mental slavery, none but ourselves can free our minds!*
>
> *Marcus Garvey*

34

FINDING A JOB AND RE-EVALUATING LIFE

Allison writes to us. Aunty Bronwyn I've had quite a hectic life and a lifestyle to match. I can't complain as I've been quite fortunate in doing more or less what I want. However, not only now have I lost my job, I've broken up with my boyfriend, I've had to move to a lesser flat than before and with no income and little else to do I just feel so alone and I've just been diagnosed with a medical condition that will need a course of lengthy regular treatments so at the moment I literally feel redundant in all areas.

Apart from job hunting, which is a job in itself dealing with all the two-faced recruitment companies, one minute they are over you like a rash the next minute next minute treating you as if you had the plague, I feel lost. Following a career today isn't like it used to be and company / employee loyalty doesn't exist except in the deceitful world of PR. I know that, because I used to put out all kinds of stuff to cover up other stuff. What to do, where to go, who indeed to speak to, big questions and no answers forthcoming.

I had a girlfriend over one evening and we were just chatting over a glass of wine – which kindly brought, and she mentioned your shows. Having all the time in the world I thought I'd at least listen to one. I think now I've listened to most of your shows and more than once. I was not only intrigued but you were so direct I felt a warmth to what you had to say. Your topics were so varied, but all had one common theme, love and common sense. You are so right when you say your world emanates from your own mind. Nowhere else does life exist except within your own thoughts and thus how you see life is all about your own perception nothing more.

It was all just so easy, no psycho-babble as you call it nothing, just plain straight forward perception. If we have a bad view on life then that's how life is, if we have a good view we smile regardless – our choice as always. It took a little time for me to get to grips with all of this even though I knew it was true, but I did.

Aunty Bronwyn where could I have gotten this information anywhere else than on your shows, it just doesn't exist. I felt so privileged that my girlfriend had shared that bit of information with me and just in passing as well. Now I'm seeing life from a totally different point of view. I still haven't got a job but I'm far more hopeful than ever. My attitude has changed and I'm challenging all the "fob offs" that I get and that has made a world of difference.

I'm seeing jobs and potential career changes now in a completely different light as I feel ready and confident to make moves that only a little while ago would have sent a shudder down my spine. I'm telling everyone I meet about your shows as I feel whatever is in their lives it could be better, and I feel it has helped me so much that I need to pass it on. Thank you so much Aunty Bronwyn for just being you, you are wonderful.

35

OUR MENTAL HEALTH

We have a letter from Edwin and he says. Aunty Bronwyn I suppose we all at times have doubts about life, and experiences of our past can loom large. At times I had been experiencing these feelings fairly often, and that was causing me concern because I couldn't just shift them. Other than that, I was feeling alright but as you say "where the mind goes the body follows" so I think it was inevitable that at certain moments mind body and soul were all at a low ebb and it's not a nice feeling.

My feelings weren't bad enough to say that I am ill, yet on the other hand it's not pleasant and takes the edge off everything you do, it also curtails your will to do things. One of your shows on Mental Health described me exactly and how I feel. I know you are not a medical MD as you point out, but I know also as much that we can talk ourselves into things or stuff, so we can talk ourselves out of it also. We just need that helping hand at times to give us that pull or push in some cases. You were saying that in many situations how we are or allow ourselves to be affects how we think, and yes, I had gotten into a low situation and yes, things thus did appear larger than they had been even though nothing had changed.

You said it's our perspective taking control as opposed to us taking control. I was just lapping all this up because it was me you were describing, and I do know Aunty Bronwyn you have been in some dire situations in your life, so I could understand exactly what you were saying and where you were coming from.

You mentioned all the self-doubt and pseudo-hysteria we concoct about ourselves and the panic that follows is often down to a dull and empty mind.

We have little else to do other than endlessly dwell upon our problems and not the solutions. That then takes over and we feel "poor old me" and then the "mind gremlins" come out to play and it's "show time". Then we hit the bottle or get tablets and moreover we needn't do either. Your shows were at times so funny I loved your eldest sister Gwyneth that alone took me out of myself, coupled with your content it brought me round and back to my senses.

Aunty Bronwyn you are the best medicine out, I think you are a tonic for everyone. I'm now enjoying life and I'll never allow myself to get back to where I was when I realised that it was me who took myself there in the first place. Big kiss Aunty Bronwyn.

Do not dwell in the past, do not dream of the future, concentrate the mind on the present moment.

Buddha

36

TAKING OWNERSHIP OF YOUR LIFE

Karl writes to us. Aunty Bronwyn it's true what you say about we can be a product of our family background. If our family are negative then we can have a tendency to be negative, if our family are positive and entrepreneurial then we can have a tendency to be like that too or at least upbeat. My family were the former, nice people but very subservient and anything that was good or successful was for "other" people, almost as if it was "too good" for them.

I didn't have any real problems in life because of this as at school I did well and automatically went forward. My parents were always pleased but at the same time sceptical that I would be too academic and end up being some weird long-haired professor or something like that. When at University things changed, I had to make sweeping decisions about my career, my likes and dislikes and choices that could be crucial to developing "me" as a person rather than just plodding forward and going with the flow.

Others seemed to just jump at opportunities whereas I could have got a Doctorate – with honours - on Procrastination. It was trying and soul destroying, I even lost girlfriends because I just couldn't get my act together, they were all bubbly and with a "go for it" attitude and I just stayed put, wondering and pondering. I was studying with a friend and over coffee she mentioned your shows and that listening to them had helped her a lot with a number of issues that she had been on her mind for some time and she said they were very funny too. I eventually got around to listening to them and one of the first topics was that on Families – just like mine.

Another evening was devoted to "Taking Ownership" and that really made me sit up and listen. You are very direct, but I like that as it has a sound quality to it and cuts out all the superfluous stuff. You said about "going with the flow" which is what I tend to do, two things go with the flow – "used toilet paper and dead fish" it not only made me smile but it is so true.

Another was respecting who I am, and casting away fears of upsetting others, as that has a tendency to put yourself down. Provided what you say or do comes from a good place then go for it. Upsetting others could be the best thing for them too to get them out of a staid and stale mind set, but that's their life not yours. Also, if others don't think the way you do it is possible you are in the wrong company, change your company to those who are on your wavelength and see how things move forward better and on a happier note.

You said lots of things Aunty Bronwyn all very good and I took them all on board too. Thank you for having the thought to broadcast your experiences it has helped me very much and I'm sure many others too. Karl.

37

LOVE AND RELIGION

June has written to us. Aunty Bronwyn what you say about Love I believe is exactly what love is all about. Where real love exists, killing and hatred, evil and corruption just can't possibly exist together. You can't have evil and love in the same place because one is dark, and one is light.

Where it all comes tumbling down as you mention is that the human being is not perfect so we get a variance where predominantly most humans are relatively good in nature but there exists a degree of negativity and many religions are just evil manifestations and nothing to do with a God of love. Also, there is now a commercial entity which adds another lesser dimension to it all. In fact, religions are man-made so there is already a flaw in the structure and ideology and the interpretation.

Similarly, in Islam for example love is so low on the agenda mass insecurity and instability, killing, violence, rape, reigns wherever it is practised and as such it offers nothing to mankind but widespread unhappiness and deceit. I really enjoyed your take on "love and religion" and have recommended it to all my friends to listen to as it puts a fresh and very real light on what we believe and how we enact our lives.

You mention that love is intrinsic to the human being and we know instinctively what love is even if we can't pin point it succinctly. Love is universal and the only thing that lets it down are personal agendas and the evilness of religions where ego overtakes love and then disharmony becomes a divisive aspect of getting along.

I love all your shows Aunty Bronwyn it's a joy to hear someone who makes sense and doesn't have any media spin to what they say.

The World is my country, all mankind are my brethren, and to do good is my religion.

Thomas Paine

38

DYSFUNCTIONAL FAMILIES

Helen has written to us Aunty Bronwyn. She says my family are dysfunctional, we hardly ever talk to one another, Christmas is a nightmare relived every year, and our parents, well I really don't know how they think if at all. Whatever my brothers and sisters do it is wrong, and they play each one of us against the other even if they have to make up stories to do so. It used to be exasperating and tiring and to some extent frustrating too as I wanted to have "nice" parents or at least parents that would have a degree of empathy towards what I do or my life, but nothing. Everything is all about them.

I have a lovely husband and two children and that for me is perfect and of course the determination as to what not to be towards my children. I may even over compensate what I do for them, but I just can't bear them growing up like I did. By chance I found that you had an App that could be downloaded onto my phone and for a long journey I was about to embark upon I though this is the entertainment I want. I wasn't disappointed Aunty Bronwyn. Each topic you mentioned was enlightening or had a different aspect to it that I enjoyed and of course your humour with your family kept making me smile especially the twins that makes me laugh just the thought of it.Your show on Dysfunctional Families I could have almost contributed to it myself, it was so so true and to the point. What you rightly said, and I should have done this, ages ago was to just move on. Take away the fantasy ideals of what parents should be like, understand they are not and probably never will be as you wish and enjoy what you have and who you have around you. One thing you did say was to say what you think to your parents, don't get upset or angry but just say what you think as and when appropriate.

I didn't call them for a long time they phoned me never asking me how I was or my husband or the two children, it just went in to an "all about me" recital. So, I told my mother that the reason I don't phone is she shows no love, she's arrogant, selfish, self- centred and I don't miss anymore talking to a cold robot that has no interest in anyone else, and if she wants to talk again try and be human or don't bother. I think she caught me out on a bad day, anyway I just went for it. I said I've got to this age have a loving family and don't need your negativity ever, so if you can't be nice there's no point in speaking. I hung up, I didn't mean to it was just a reaction.

My mother phoned back but I didn't pick up the phone. The next time she phoned was as if nothing had happened, but she did ask me how I was and Bob and the two children, all very much a matter of fact but she did it. Maybe, just maybe she has melted a bit from the "ice queen" she was. Anyway, Aunty Bronwyn, thank you for your lovely Shows, ideal listening with a cup of tea hearing you always rejuvenates me. Thank you again.

39

WHY AM I BULLIED?

William writes to us. Aunty Bronwyn bullying is a complex thing, people can be picked upon for a whole range of reasons many of which are not evident in their motives to many others. However, it is not only very real it is something that is cruel and very harmful. Children driven to desperation by being bullied have committed suicide because to them at their age they just cannot see an end to it or to how life can get better. It's also a big stigma on themselves as to why it happens and the understanding or lack of it by those around them including parents and teachers. Plus, the fact that they are perpetually frightened that if they do say anything there will be recriminations that will lead to worse things at some time or other both outside the home and school surroundings. i.e. it cannot be at all policed.

Young people are still immature and very easily lead and follow others as they like to feel "in" with a crowd or group, they haven't as yet developed or understand that they can be "individuals" in fact in many cases it still frightens them, even if they are loudmouths. I was bullied at school and life was hell, I was in tears every day at home and dreaded getting up every morning. At playtime I hung around the inside of the school so that I would be near a staff member or it would ward off the bullies coming forward.

This worked more or less but it was tactical, and it solved nothing, the threat was very real and always there, life remained permanently on alert and was incredibly stressful.

I by chance heard your programme on bullying and it brought it all back, not in a negative way but the struggle I had and how I had overcome it, as you rightly say it is purely education because you will never ever be able to stop it before it starts because it often starts out as something slightly arrogant and then before you know it, it is bullying.

Getting other children to report it anonymously is an ideal way as they can spot it a mile away far before teachers and parents. Making the game plans transparent places an ownership on pupils and who they are so they take control without being heroic or standing out and fearing repercussions of being grilled to the nth degree.

Your programme was very comforting, and I've mentioned it to a few parents to listen to as it was so very real in every way. Thank you, Aunty Bronwyn for your input and taking the stigma out of bullying, it has and I'm sure will make a difference to others lives.

Never be bullied into silence. Never allow yourself to be made a victim. Accept no one's definition of your life; define yourself.

Harvey Fierstein

40

DRUGS
THE PIT TO NOWHERE

Aunty Bronwyn Stephan has written to us. Aunty Bronwyn Drug abuse is nothing new and there is very little else to say other than it's just pathetic and stupid and a waste of a life and a great distress to those around. I'm not a drug user nor have I been but my brother was and as you mentioned there is nothing a drug user won't do to get a fix. They will lie, cheat, steal, you name it to obtain money by any means and you just can't trust what they will do next, completely erratic in thought and logic but at all times totally self-centred.

I've been listening to your shows for some time now and the one on Drug Abuse rang home very clearly as it was the epitome of my brother who has sadly passed away now. He was loved by us all and a bright quick-witted guy, always laughing playing jokes, good fun to be with, a perfect bother and son. He moved away from home to get a job in an advertising agency in London. We were all very pleased because he was getting a very handsome salary for his creative abilities, and I'll say one thing he was excellent at what he did, and he did a few things for me which were brilliant.

I went to stay with him one holiday and was so excited until I arrived at his luxury flat. It was a tip, it was not like him at all. He was moody, irascible, quite sharp with me at times something I'd never seen in him before. We went out and had some great meals and met some of his friends who seemed very nice, but he wasn't himself. Holiday over I told my parents I had a ball and left it at that.

He eventually came home for a weekend to see the folks and he had aged 20 years and was so skinny, my parents were shocked but said nothing.

The weekend was an ordeal and he said he had to go to a couple of meetings nearby which was odd. but we later found out it was for his fix. He went back to London and the next thing he had lost his job and was on a drug programme, but I fear that was all too late as he had lost the will because shortly after the police phoned advising us of his death.

Aunty Bronwyn none of us are angels and I know you have had a good life all over the world I also know you have seen rock bottom too which you have mentioned. I think your show needs to be heard by others as it outlines that taking drugs is a road to nowhere, it turns people into worthless zombies with a death wish at the end.

I got my parents to listen to your show and whilst it brought back memories for them it still kept the love which is never lost alive and hope that others will not succumb to the cheap thrill of taking drugs that eventually grabs a hold and never let's go. Thank you, Aunty Bronwyn.

41

LONELINESS IS IT A CHOICE OR NOT?

Amanda has written to us and says. Aunty Bronwyn I'm a social worker for the local council and look after the community welfare programme predominantly for the elderly but not exclusively. I see many people from all walks of life and situations as to why they are where they are and hopefully we can make life a little better for them in some way or other.

I heard your show on loneliness the other day and I think you hit it spot on where many lonely people are concerned. That loneliness for many is self-generated because of real meanness within. They just don't give of themselves it's not financial but just themselves, they apportion everything in life as if it is on a check list, you do this, I do that, you do this, I do that, you don't do this therefore I'm not going to do that, and they are really adamant in sticking rigidly to this thought. Even phone calls, I phoned them, they need to phone me now, and so it goes on.

Yet many of those who are disabled are ten times happier and have such a warm heart and have a whole load of friends because they just give out the warmth they have which is always welcoming. You are right too when you say the lonely are predominantly closed minded and full of excuses like. "I keep to myself" a common expression which means I'm not helping anyone. Another common saying "You're lucky there aren't any nice people around here", which means no matter where you are you'll never entertain anyone because it will mean exerting yourself.

Aunty Bronwyn you are so right in what you have to say about loneliness becoming a way of life and people lose the ability to communicate. I'm even saying all this to many people now, it shocks them yes, but they know it's all true. I've gotten everyone in my department to listen to your show on Loneliness as I think it is a worthwhile listen. Thank you, Aunty Bronwyn.

Pray that your loneliness may spur you into finding something to live for, great enough to die for.

Dag Hammarskjold

42

SAYING NO – OFTEN A DIFFICULT THING TO DO

Aunty Bronwyn Paul writes to us. Aunty Bronwyn I've really found it difficult to say no. I think it has a lot to do with my upbringing and with few exceptions I've just said yes to everything then regretted it and had to email or text afterwards saying no. Sometimes however that isn't possible, and I've then had to go on to do something that I didn't want to do.

I heard your show on "saying no" and it gave me a bit more courage to muster the ability to say No, I don't want to do this. Sometimes as you say, saying NO and adding just a little more like "No, I don't want to do this" and not be drawn into a conversation as to why. i.e. No means No. Much of it has to do with respecting yourself I know and at times that awful feeling of guilt or letting others down or worse still "what will others think". As you rightly say, you are in charge of your life not others, so they can think what they like, they are most definitely not perfect themselves that's for sure.

I've started where appropriate to say no and look at whoever it is in the eye when I say it. It does make a difference, and if challenged not to be drawn into their conversation for themselves or make up an elaborate story just to appease them, they have no right (except in a few cases) to question you as such and they should respect you. Also, some people are quite selfish and bombastic and talk loudly hoping to intimidate you to get you to do what they want. But if you are going to say No say it with some force, and if you have to repeat it say No the second time even more loudly with a slight annoying edge to your voice, your body language should then kick in to physically affirm your resounding No!

You were very right too Aunty Bronwyn that many try to use "emotional blackmail" to get you to do something by saying "If you don't do this you'll be letting everyone down" which is usually the biggest pack of lies out. If you died whatever it was would continue without you anyway. Stand your ground and the more you do so the better you get at throwing the whole scenario back to them as inappropriate. That is "I've said no". I'm getting better at this Aunty Bronwyn and I feel so good when I've said No to something, it has boosted my self-esteem no end. Thank you for your show Aunty Bronwyn, it was all very simple even if a bit nerve racking at first, but step by step I'm really getting there.

> *Who you are speaks so loudly I can't hear what you're saying.*
>
> *Ralph Waldo Emerson*

43

STOP WAITING FOR APPROVAL

We have a letter from Pierre who says. Aunty Bronwyn you often say that you could well be a product of your upbringing good or bad. Good if you are well mannered but bad if you lose the push you need in life because your parents didn't possess it. Well this was me I was the person you were talking about. I knew that I had to do something otherwise my dreams and aspirations would come to nothing and I would only have myself to blame.

I'm over 18, so technically and legally I have every opportunity to change my life and not just sit there and blame my parents and leave it at that. And anyway – they are not bad parents but have little push in life. As you put it, it would be the soft option and an idiot's way to living their life to blame what was the past when you have the knowledge to change the present for the future to evolve. As you also mentioned many people hold on to the past as an excuse for not going forward or failing, they are already failures and pathetic ones too and have a great deal of selfishness because they always need an audience to plagiarise with their story – emotional vampires. It's difficult to snap out of years of waiting for those mythical people or bodies to say "Yes" or "Go ahead" because it smacks of giving away your authority to others who have literally no say at all in whether you do something or not.

It's almost like you need a pat on the back just for the sake of it to make you feel good. All what you said Aunty Bronwyn was just me to a T, it was actually quite embarrassing to an extent as if you had read my mind. It does require a new way of thinking, and I decided to do it, I just went my way and started with my business project and you know with few exceptions you need very little acceptance at all to do almost anything you want, you just do it. It's amazing how tangled your mind can get when you build up these mythical bodies or anonymous people of control, they don't exist.

My own business venture is now underway, I have staff and I am developing new strategies all the time and I'm loving it. My parents can't get to grips with it and always remark on what I used to be like. Aunty Bronwyn, just a thank you for your radio broadcast on Taking Ownership, it was the seed which I planted, and it germinated into what it is. I've recommended all my friends to listen to your shows. All the best Pierre.

> *A truly strong person does not need the approval of others any more than a lion needs the approval of sheep.*
>
> *Vernon Howard*

44

MENTAL HEALTH – MIDDLE EAST

Afina has written to us. Aunty Bronwyn I'm your number one fan in the Middle East I live in Saudi Arabia with my family. At the moment I'm in London with them which I love London too much. It's difficult for women in the Middle East even me with my family and they are quite liberal but at the same time I have to be careful in what I do and say. For women to get on it can be so difficult and frustrating, especially when I see the girls in London dressing nicely and going out on their own, it is just a fantasy in Saudi Arabia, is there any wonder we are such a backward country and it never gets anywhere.

At times I think I'm going to go out of my mind, being brought up as a prisoner doing nothing, no intellectual conversation and just being lumped together with other Saudi girls who are either like me or even worse. No one is interested or cares about Saudi women we were born women and that's it, in Islam you are nothing but a man's possession and in Saudi it stays like that.

There are a few women who break free, but their parents are probably more enlightened, the rest of us can only go so far or do so much and we can't travel freely. If a woman is seen alone she is regarded as being loose even after being covered up, it's pathetic. I would so like to meet you Aunty Bronwyn as I think you are so interesting and a few of my friends would like to meet you too I know.

It would be such an honour for us if you could come to Saudi Arabia.

Listening to you has given me a great deal of comfort and hope and I hope one day to marry a man who will take me to London to live. Even the magazines in Saudi have pages torn out or blacked over with fibre pen so we can't see things such is the censorship even today. Without your Shows, Aunty Bronwyn I don't know what I would do I dream of just doing a few things you mention, and I listen In my room on my mobile phone so that no one will know or find out. Thank you, Aunty Bronwyn love from Afina.

> **A woman is like a tea bag - you can't tell how strong she is until you put her in hot water.**
>
> *Eleanor Roosevelt*

45

MY DISABILITY – MY LIFE

Aunty Bronwyn, Mike has written with the following. Aunty Bronwyn I was diagnosed with a degenerative illness when in my late teens. For a while everything was basically OK then bit by bit I had to stop doing things until eventually I couldn't even walk and needed a wheelchair. I then started losing strength in my upper limbs and got so worried that I would just end up with no movement at all.

Fortunately, with today's technology and drugs I can still move my arms and hands and for that I really have to be grateful. Of course, fewer friends come to see me; I can't meet them or actively even meet for a pizza or a glass of wine so that has curtailed much of my social activity and mental stimulus. I was already an ardent follower of yours Aunty Bronwyn I had even meant to write to you but never did. However, on your show Taking Ownership you said don't ever allow yourself to go down the "poor old me syndrome" route ever, no matter how bad things are, just stand clear of all of that. That actually rang a bell with me because to be honest I have come to a place a few times feeling so low that I nearly went down that route, but never did.

You went on to say reinventing your life isn't an option it's a necessity and you will find both the courage and ingenuity within you if you once start to try. You also said just because when you start you will probably draw blanks and it then all appears to mean nothing you just keep on because that makes success all that much sweeter. I did just that, I could hear your voice in my mind saying it over and over again and persevered even though I had a few really down days.

Aunty Bronwyn you are magic, you were so right after an age of phoning and emailing I got one positive reply, and again you were right the first few negative calls were almost practice calls because I modified my banter so much that eventually I hit the right tone and speech. I have a home job which is not only brilliant it gives me a good wage so that I can buy all the gadgets and stuff I want to. I can get out more now too. All of this has given me new friends and that has cheered me up no end, I'm living a life again.

Thank you, Aunty Bronwyn just for your words of wisdom. I know deep down how you must have gone through hard times in the past but pulled yourself out by what you have said. Big hug Aunty Bronwyn and thank you again, Mike.

> *I enjoy convalescence.*
> *It is the part that makes*
> *the illness worth while.*
>
> *George Bernard Shaw*

46

DEATH – WHEN IT HITS YOU HARD

Aunty Bronwyn Hillary writes to us. Aunty Bronwyn, it is just such a pity we aren't all taught at school about death and dying. I know it is not the most uplifting of subjects but no matter what age you are it is going to affect you one way or another sooner or later. When you are young the world is still your oyster and life can one day be depressing and another day you are over the moon. However, as you get older life levels out a bit and you see things differently, and life has different values and you appreciate things that when younger had little meaning at all.

I was at sixth form at school my sister died from leukaemia and shortly after my mother with breast cancer. I could have filled an ocean with tears, I just switched off completely from life and whilst my father did his best he was suffering too and was trying his as well as he could to stay buoyant and together. The family were supportive, but all lived miles away from us and thus couldn't physically help. Some neighbours were amazingly helpful especially as my father had occasionally to travel abroad on business. In the meantime, however there was me thinking, why, why, why, what's it all mean and that was the recurring theme in my mind, I just couldn't turn it off.

Bit by bit you do come to terms with what's happened, but it still leaves that massive void in the pit of your stomach that needs quenching. If there is a God, then why? If there isn't a God, then what's it all about? Is there in fact a middle ground that I don't know about? The endless questions overtaking my life and making me feel like I was in a bubble just waiting for it to burst and then all would be alright. It wouldn't, how could it, but that's how it felt. I felt bitter in a sort of way, yet I couldn't relay that thought it was just something inner something deep down that was irksome.

I started Aunty Bronwyn listening to your shows at a neighbour's house when my father went abroad for ten days. My friend's mother used to listen to them and I actually looked forward to sitting down with her and listening to the letters of other people and we used to comment and laugh afterwards at your family and the twins and what people had put up with in life. One evening you spoke on Bereavement and it really made such a difference. I like it also because you just say what you think and that in itself is cathartic because few people do.

I just love the way you talk about how pathetic our religious leaders are they can't explain anything about anything. You however did explain about the love element and that was so moving, I could feel and hear my mother and my sister and suddenly it all fell into place. I know they won't come back but they are now at rest and still with me in my mind.

When my father came back I got him to listen to the programme too, it also made a difference to him and as a family of two now we are a better team and coping better also. You are so right Aunty Bronwyn it is often the simplest of things that make the biggest difference and what you had to say in a few minutes spoke volumes. Love is the only thing that matters because without it you are nothing. Thank you so much, Aunty Bronwyn you have put the sun back into my life. Lots of love Hillary.

47

WHERE SUCCESS LIES – WITHIN YOU

Dan has written to us. Aunty Bronwyn, I wasn't all that good at school, I did OK but definitely no Einstein. I didn't go to University I didn't even go into an apprenticeship scheme because I just couldn't think what to do. I was always good at tinkering around with things and making things work but that's hardly a profession. I used to like cooking and was always creating stuff at home most of which my parents liked although I did have a few famous catastrophes, I supposed it's the learning curve.

By chance I met someone who was a friend of a friend of mine and we just seemed to hit it off as mates straight away as he seemed to see life exactly as I did. Over some time, we got to know each other better and spoke more personally and openly and eventually came up with a plan to sell specialist food from a van. For weeks we cooked together and devised a menu based upon the locations we had in mind, or even to follow construction sites to provide hot tasty food.
We also followed the American idea of Twittering our days location ahead so that people would know in advance.

My mate's sister used to listen to your shows and one evening we were in and she was listening to it, far from being a soppy show we thought it would be it was great and really informative and funny. Your programme on Taking Ownership just got us both so motivated that we could do anything the only thing stopping us was ourselves.

This is so true, we were both motivated by each other to start our enterprise but what you had to say really set us on fire and we just did it. It took some time as we had to work in between to finance it all, but it was just such fun. We are now starting our second van and who knows what else may happen. Thanks Aunty Bronwyn if you ever around come and have a free meal on us. Dan and Tommy.

> ***Success is not the key to happiness.***
> ***Happiness is the key to success.***
> ***If you love what you are doing,***
> ***you will be successful.***
>
> ***Albert Schweitzer***

48

FAMILIES ARE STRANGE – NOT BEING EQUAL

Aunty Bronwyn Emily writes to us. Aunty Bronwyn, I come from a family of four, two sisters and a brother and me. I can't say that I have had a bad childhood but from an early age I always seemed to be the "odd one" out in the family. I always seemed to get less than my brothers and sisters even when I said so there was always an answer, but that was never enough.

Over time I accepted that and even my brothers and sisters accepted that I got less. It is strange to say what and why, but it was always as if I was the one imposing on the rest or excess to the family. This had an impact on me in that I felt for want of saying it "not wanted" or "inferior". Even when I was outside, and things were being given out I nearly always expected when it came to my turn there wouldn't be anything left, or it would be broken or there would be some excuse as to why I couldn't have it.

I had in mind that life for me would be just like that. By chance I heard a number your programmes Taking Ownership, Life is Not Equal, and a few others and bit by bit I realised that whatever was happening it was nothing to do with me. As you said Aunty Bronwyn, how people treat you or see you is their perception, it hasn't made you any less or more of a person than you already are. Life is as it is, it is us that makes it what it is for ourselves. I suddenly stopped feeling inferior and my whole attitude changed. There was an incident where there were some treats for each of us and I saw only three, so as I was near the table I took one, my mother came up quickly to me and as she got close I looked at her and said, "yes". She apologised to my brother and said she had made a mistake and would get some more for him. That was some time ago now. Since then I have been bold in a quiet way and it has really paid off, although slightly disconcerting to my parents and not ideal to myself.

I've met a fabulous man and we are to get married, he's also quite wealthy too as it happens and has lovely parents and two other brothers both of whom are married. The protocol of families meeting and getting together all came into play so one evening at my boyfriend's house I just told them about the years of being second best – I had mentioned this to my boyfriend already, just to get everything out in the open, as you said Aunty Bronwyn why hide other's shortcomings it's for them to deal with not you to carry around as if guilty yourself.

They were somewhat taken back but when they met my parents went overboard about how privileged they were to have me in their family, it was so nice to hear someone saying something nice about me and I know it was true his family are very nice indeed. I'm not sure what prompted her, but my mother said that I was always special, and I replied, "that's true".

Then she said what a nice girl I had been, so I said quietly "stop drinking mother you are making it all up".

I don't want to fall out with my parents, I don't have bad feelings for them but after over twenty years of being second best it does take its toll.

But Aunty Bronwyn you are so right what goes around etc, and speak the truth, don't harbour others negativity as if it's your own dark secret. You don't have to make a scene out of anything but just that levelling of the playing field can make a world of difference and it has and thank you for sharing that thought. It may have taken me a while to get there but I have and I'm really looking forward to my life ahead. Thank you, Aunty Bronwyn.

No one can make you feel inferior without your consent.

Eleanor Roosevelt

49

MIDDLE AGED AND CONFUSED

Aunty Bronwyn Beryl writes in to say. Aunty Bronwyn, I'm middle aged single, unemployed and was quite confused as to what to do with my life. I've had a good and global life. I've been lucky to travel the world and enjoy nice places, food, clothes almost a bit of a jet set existence with the exception that I wasn't really, I was working, never the less it was fun. When one starts out one doesn't think of the end it's as if that is some mythical or fictitious point in time. But that time does and has arrived. Regardless of your looks, knowledge experience etc there are always new and exciting people just like I was queuing up to take your place. In enjoying my lifestyle, I gave up the opportunity of marriage a couple of times and with that a possibility of a family, although I've never been a child orientated type of person.

It is just so sobering when it all comes tumbling down and all that's left are memories. Sat in my flat still with a healthy tan, sipping cups of tea and staring into a nothingness thinking, "What am I going to do now"? How could I possibly match what I have just been doing. Three days in from my last First-Class flight and that's the end of the road for this part of my life. A girlfriend of mine came over and she started talking about your shows, so I thought I'd listen. They were all very good and I'm now a fan but the one that attracted my attention was "Taking Ownership" of your life. The first thing was "don't go down that poor old me route" whatever you do. No sighs, or shaking of the head or anything else, just stay on top. No muttering to yourself and no looking back either, the route is always forward, you're not going any other way.

The next thing isn't to compare what was to what might be otherwise you hold on to intransigent stuff which no more has meaning. The other thing you said was dress appropriately as to where you want to go or be, be that person even if only at this time in your mind. Seek other opportunities and don't hold back saying what you want, at the same time don't take on board the weird looks or lack of real contact that you may get from those who are supposedly trying to help. Their lack of ability or creative desire could be totally lost, and they will possibly view you as someone who is seeking what's not there, even though there is something there even if it's not known at that time. It was your real determination that got to me Aunty Bronwyn because I know you have had to re-invent yourself and have been a success at it.

I did all you said and for a while nothing happened, but I thought OK, I'm not going to get depressed I've planted those seeds, just give it time and carry on. I got two calls almost in a row of amazing jobs. Either are mine, I'm just making up my mind now. Thank you for your encouragement Aunty Bronwyn it really does make a difference and I would recommend anyone to listen to you. Thanks again. Beryl.

50

OLDER / YOUNGER GAY RELATIONSHIP

Aunty Bronwyn Barry has sent us this message. Aunty Bronwyn I came out quite late in life having previously been married. I am 54 and have two grown up children. I can't say that I was actively looking for a partner, but I enjoyed my new gay friends and life was OK.

I socialised, had meals, holidays, etc and that was all fine and at least I laughed. I had a couple of "flings" but it was no more than that and I had resolved my-self to life just as it was. On holiday with three of my friends we met on an excursion a bunch of younger guys in their twenties who all seemed fun and up for anything that was going. One of which I got on very well with which was not only nice but very flattering too. At the end of the excursion and a few drinks later he asked which hotel I was staying in and my contact details in the UK, I gave him my mobile number.

I heard no more, and it seemed like a distant memory. When I was back home he eventually phoned which took me by surprise. Evidently, he and his friends contacted gastroenteritis on another excursion as did the whole coach party. Long story short. We met up, just got on like a house on fire, he has been living with me now for three months and it's another life I never thought that could or even would have existed. We both have very good jobs so there's no financial leverage of any kind.

Aunty Bronwyn I listened to your shows a lot when I was going through my divorce, it helped me enormously even just looking at life differently too which I now had to do. On your shows you had letters from other gay guys who had had some very heavy life experiences and coped. Also, your base line is that of love, for with love we can overcome or accept anything and stop yourself analysing your life let it be what it is. All of your shows were really very good for we never get training or are prepared for what may transpire in life, things just happen, and we cope, sometimes very badly.

I had to psych myself up to get to grips with Justin moving in with me and I can honestly say I heard your voice in my mind saying, "the only thing stopping you is you" and that decided it all, and I'm so glad it happened. Also, the fact you said in one of your shows "your life is yours – always – never let others hijack it for any reason". This was a big step for me but WOW I'm loving it. Aunty Bronwyn thank you so much. Big hugs Barry & Jason.

Our prime purpose in this life is to help others. And if you can't help them, at least don't hurt them.

Dalai Lama

51

INFIDELITY / UNFAITHFULNESS – A STEP TOO FAR (1)

Aunty Bronwyn we have received two letters almost identical about being unfaithful here is the first from Claire. Aunty Bronwyn you often say that there are two things in life you must and mustn't do. One is you must step over the imaginary line in your own life to achieve something. The other is not to step over the line when it comes to another people's trust. I have done both and, in the process, I have become a winner and a loser.

Many years ago, I started an accessory business for women, very distinctive styles but then I knew the market I was aiming for. My husband supported me and indeed set up the office for me as he has expertise in that area. It was a struggle to get off the ground but again one of your favourite expressions "never ever give up regardless". I didn't give up and it all of a sudden took off.

At a networking meeting I met a man who sourced clothing and accessory products for overseas markets and that became very lucrative and financially very rewarding. I was subsequently invited to a number of overseas markets and that's where it all went wrong. I was suddenly introduced to an almost "jet set" life in an instant and an affair started. I knew it was wrong, but I just couldn't say no as I was in a wash with my new status.

You also say quite often very little happens in isolation and indeed the tell-tale singes started to break through.

My husband was devastated as he was so proud of my achievements, but he was just too shattered overall and went to stay with our daughter for a short spell, he just couldn't bear to see me for a while. We are now divorced, finance agreed amicably, and are reasonable friends, the children keep us somewhat in touch. I'm full of regret I could have had it all, nice family, husband, lifestyle - everything you could wish for really. Aunty Bronwyn I wish I had taken your advice and not just listened to it. One stupid mistake but it was definitely a deliberate mistake and that's it.

You pay for your mistakes in life one way or another. I'm just writing to say that I hope other people in my position think twice before embarking on an episode of self-important arrogance because there is 'no reset' button in life. Best wishes Claire.

Love is understood, in a historical way, as one of the great human vocations - but its counterspell has always been infidelity. This terrible, terrible betrayal that can tear apart not only another person, not only oneself, but whole families.

Junot Diaz

52

INFIDELITY / UNFAITHFULNESS – A STEP TOO FAR (2)

The second letter is from Clarke about his experience. Aunty Bronwyn I have been listening to your broadcasts for some time now and I agree with just about everything you have to say. I have an excellent job and was out of the blue promoted to a quite senior position with benefits. My wife and I moved to a larger and better house and there we had two wonderful children. My promotions didn't stop and very soon I became in charge of a number of overseas territories which meant protracted periods of time away from home, but it did pay for a very good lifestyle for us.

Despite the opportunities to be unfaithful overseas I resisted it all and felt just so good as the last thing I wanted to do was hurt my wife in any way. Then I met this young "girl about town" at a company event and my senses left me. She was the life and soul of life itself, my ego had never been elevated and the classic thing started buying new trendy clothes and the lot. Well, the bubble burst, my wife found out, everyone always finds out no matter what you do and that was it. Lots of unpleasant times ensued, divorce was imminent, and I now have a great job but no wife who I deeply loved and now have a 'lads' social life which isn't very good.

I tried to make amends but even those who love you back when you break their heart you literally can't mend it like it was. Aunty Bronwyn, you say so many good and wise things and it all sounds good, but we tend to push it to the back of our minds thinking it won't happen, until it does, and then it's all too late.

We all think we are smart and can overrule the rules in life, but we can't. I hope Aunty Bronwyn that those others listening to your shows will take note, there is no room for stupidity in life. Best Clarke.

Infidelity is a deal breaker for me. I've broken up with people over it. You can't do monogamy 90 percent of the time.

Alanis Morissette

53

ADDICTED TO SEX - MALE (1)

Aunty Bronwyn we have had a number of letters from people who have said they are addicted to sex, here are two. The first one is from Keith. Aunty Bronwyn I like to think that I am quite a normal guy in every respect, I'm single, I like sports and like going out with the lads, but I was constantly thinking about sex. Whereas my mates see girls and talk about then I 'm out there going for the pull and it gets to the stage where if it is getting late I don't even care what they look like as long as I can just have sex. To be honest it was getting me down and it was even getting my mates down too because it seemed to them that it was becoming a habit. What is even worse is that when I see who I've been with I really feel ashamed of both myself and that some of the girls have let themselves become like they have, almost worthless.

On one of your programmes on Sex and Relationships you said there are two areas that can cause this, other than a possible high sex drive. One is the one you create yourself then it becomes habitual and the other it is because you have some psychological aspect that needs to be fulfilled yet it never is. I dwelt on this for a while and I thought it was the former as I never used to be like this and if I'm in an all-male environment like in sports I don't miss it at all. It's this ego conquest thing but it has such a big let-down factor afterwards.

After pondering much over what you had said I thought I'm never going to get a girlfriend as the ones I really like don't want to know me, I have to change who I am. I gave myself a week without sex then two and I did actually after that see both sex and girls in a different light.

It's amazing how I had blinded myself. It didn't stop the urges, but it was easier to control. My pathetic chat up lines vanished, I actually started talking to girls and they started answering back positively as opposed to walking away and telling their friends who the moron was who had tried chatting her up.

It's amazing how we can let ourselves go and fall fowl of our own negative emotions. Thank you, Aunty Bronwyn it has made just such a drastic change, who would have ever thought having too much sex could be a handicap, but it can.

*Sex is a part of nature.
I go along with nature.*

Marilyn Monroe

54

ADDICTED TO SEX – FEMALE (2)

This second letter is from Miriam. Aunty Bronwyn, I used to be such a timid girl and the suddenly developed this taste for constant sex. I just didn't care who, when, where it was sex for the sake of it. I didn't have any men friends but loads of lovers of the "instant" variety. I don't know what happened or why, well I suppose I know why, it's just that longing to be needed even if it's just for a matter of minutes. That constant emotional fix that does nothing but destroy your life. I used to think prostitution was cheap and nasty until I realised I was just as bad or even worse.

I heard your show on Sex and Relationships and I thought that's me you are talking about, no excuses, I'm the sex for sex sake person you are describing. You were right too I had few friends and no hope whatsoever of ever having a boyfriend, who wants a slut as a girlfriend. The realisation wasn't hard but stopping it was. Sex was a habit, it was a drug, it was my fix, something that was a reason to do things or plan for no matter what or who.

I had to psych myself up but I did refrain from sex and from going out except to the cinema or a meal. I had to literally keep away from pubs or clubs or gatherings of any kind. I can tell you now of every TV show on the box, but it did start to work. Bit by bit I allowed myself to wean my habit slowly from its number one focus to something obscure.

It took a matter of months to really start to feel the benefit and already I'm putting the past behind me as if it hadn't happened and really look forward to meeting a nice guy – something that I can't remember who they were.

Aunty Bronwyn, thank you for your shows. They do do some good believe me, not only have I gotten over this awful phase but I've even healed the rift with my parents because of what you have said, and on my terms too. Thank you, Aunty Bronwyn you are an Angel…

> **Sex without love is a meaningless experience, but as far as meaningless experiences go, its pretty damn good.**
>
> *Woody Allen*

55

PERMISSION, APPROVAL, VALIDATION (1)

Aunty Bronwyn we have a letter here from Anthony who is telling us about how he overcame his shyness and feelings of subservience. Aunty Bronwyn you often mention that we are a product of our parents' behaviour and / or environment and that in our teens / later life we have the fee will to change that. I would have argued that a while ago and said "you don't know my situation" as if everything and everyone else had a hand in what I did or said.

Well, the truth is they did have a hand in what I did or said because I not only invited it into my life I allowed it to happen too then it became part of my life. I was getting really fed up with life until I heard your Show on Taking Ownership. It really did hit a note deep within that my problems were mine no one else lives in my mind so I can't blame these mythical events to control it any more, it's just a really cheap cop out. All your other Shows I had negative opinions on too, but you know Aunty Bronwyn I knew you were right but to admit it would have rocked my world.

It is said there's a time and a place well that was a while ago, I had to admit who I was to myself, what were my main problems, and just take ownership. It was a double shock to the system, firstly, getting to grips with myself and changing my attitude.

Secondly, all those around me who had gotten used to telling me stuff and me like a little dog following on behind.

Many of whom of course actually I didn't like. This was also an eye opener for me too, that my so- called friends and so called loving family weren't so friendly and weren't so loving.

Aunty Bronwyn you have an answer for everything, as I had listened to many of your shows and you had mentioned about putting yourself first, being number one, because if you aren't number one then you can't look after others either. A few sleepless nights later, but with determination and going over your shows again and again as my mantra I thought this is it. So, I literally took a deep breath and said what I wanted (you also said just go for it even if your legs are wobbling and your voice is weak, just do it) so I did it. Well my legs were wobbling. and I lost the depth of my voice, it being raised an octave I think but I heard your voice so clearly in my minds thoughts pushing me on so I thought "I'm doing this".

You are so right, to live my life I don't need permission, validation nor approval from anyone whatsoever, I am me that's enough of all of those three things to get me through to do just what I want. I'm so pleased I listened to your shows because the backlash was amazing, the selfishness of others wanting to control you or having had that ability and now it's gone they just couldn't really get to grips with it at all.

But expecting this I was verbally armed although as you pointed out silence at times makes the loudest noise. For a while I think looking back I was a bit of an ogre, but that's calmed down now.

My life is a million times better and I'm seeking another job and have a few new and better friends and doing things like I never did before including going to the gym which I love. Thank you, Aunty Bronwyn you have really helped me transform my life and given me a new perspective. God Bless you are a real Wonder Woman.... Anthony.

> ***I much prefer the sharpest criticism of a single intelligent man to the thoughtless approval of the masses.***
>
> ***Johannes Kepler***

56

PERMISSION, APPROVAL, VALIDATION (2)

We have a letter from Ajay who writes. Aunty Bronwyn I come from quite a large Asian family. I can't say anything bad about my upbringing because we were all looked after well and had every chance at school and university. However, like a lot of Asian families our family has more baggage than an airport on a busy day.

The "unwritten" do's and don't's and 'what will the family think' or 'the neighbours' or 'the community' is legendary, yet in today's environment it lives purely in the mind and serves no purpose. You often say that you can be a product of your family / environment well that can be just so true. Two of my brothers and sisters have married and moved away and are so different now, completely different people having broken away from the confining and narrow home environment.

We are taught to respect our families but as you rightly point out respect has to be earned it is not bestowed no matter who you are. As Asians we are British and live in the UK not some small village in India, yet the mentality is not far from that. All of my brothers and sisters went to University and that opens your eyes to the "bigger picture" another of your sayings Aunty Bronwyn. We have had our fair share of family arguments as to who has permission to marry who, but it never held as my brother and sister both said if you don't like it don't turn up.

Aunty Bronwyn what really hits the mark is what you constantly say about "if love is present then everything is possible" and "what more can a parent want for their child than their happiness"?

Yet stupid protocols and pathetic old cultures have nothing whatsoever within them about love, nothing. The bottom line is I am marrying a white girl. My brothers and sisters get on well with her and vice versa too. We have been going out together for three years. I'm getting from my father and aunties all this "it will upset your mother and what will the family think" and I reply. "I don't care, I'm not giving up my future wife for my mother throwing a designer selfish fit to make things fit into her little world", which I've made clear.

You are so right Aunty Bronwyn, no one needs Permission, Approval or Validation to live, you are a unique entity in yourself and that is perfect just as it is. What we do need more of are not rules but loads of love, sadly that seems to be the last thing on the list not the first.

Thank you, Aunty Bronwyn for your broadcasts, listening to them just gave me that push that I needed and that's worth such a lot. We are sending an invitation to you for the wedding. Big hugs Ajay.

57

CHOICES (1)

We have a letter here from Tunde he says. Aunty Bronwyn I first listened to your show in Nigeria, it's amazing what you can pick up on the radio channels these days on your mobile phone. I had no idea what it was or who you were, but it just sounded interesting, so I listened. What a revelation, and I know now you have been to Nigeria also, so you have an idea about how people think and speak out there.

I am now in the UK and have a very good job and enjoying myself. It is a different culture in the UK and the way people think and talk is far more upbeat and positive. I just wish I could bottle what you have to say Aunty Bronwyn and market it in Lagos, we would both be very wealthy. Life is a series of choices as you say frequently, and you are so right. You can't always dictate what circumstances you are in or the parameters in which you live and work, but what you are in charge of yourself 24/7 and you choose to move within those areas accordingly. No one else can do it for you. Even if you get help or assistance you still have to walk the walk and many people don't even do that just wanting everything on a plate.

You are a very strong lady Aunty Bronwyn, holding on to taking control of your life and not letting others take it away from you. Listening to your shows is one of the highlights of the week for me, I feel so revitalised and uplifted. I like your family too, they shocked me at first, but I love them now they have grown on me. Thank you, Aunty Bronwyn Tunde.

58

CHOICES (2)

A letter from Paul, he writes. Aunty Bronwyn you'd think getting married would be exciting, fabulous and all the things you wanted for. Well it is, and it isn't all in the same breath. My girlfriend and I are to get married, this is what I want more than anything and she too, that we are both adamant about. When it comes to the dress and bridesmaids and anything else I'm really more than happy she does what she wants I don't care as long as she is happy that's fine. I'd even wear a pink suite on the day if it pleased her, it's just the one day and my brother would do the same – I think!!!

Up until now both sets of parents have gotten on well, no problems there until now the planning of the wedding, they are like two sumo wrestlers grappling to see who can outdo the other and win the contest, so they can have their way. One evening my girlfriend and I were discussing the wedding, which was getting a bit tense now, although we did have to laugh at who we thought was getting married us or our parents? My girlfriend suddenly jumped up and said "Aunty Bronwyn" I wondered what she was talking about but then she said listen to this.

The show was on Choices, and it certainly put into perspective what we had to do. It's often not that you don't know what to do it is just listening to someone else say it that affirms your mind, especially if like you Aunty Bronwyn who doesn't mince her words.

It is our wedding, so our choices go, if our decisions happen to be as our parents fine, if not that's fine too. One thing is for sure we are getting married full stop. We decided that we would now take charge feeling confident in our roles as it was now becoming a feud and not a wedding arrangement. I (we) told both parents this is what we are doing, and this is how we are doing it, because it is our wedding not theirs. Both parties were uneasy and couldn't say much but that's for them to get over. All went well in the end it was a good day. Both parents back on speaking terms too and I didn't have to wear pink either – whew!!!

Aunty Bronwyn it was so good to hear you talk because apart from the sentiments going around in my mind, your independent take on Choices and Taking Charge was so vitalising that it clarified everything in an instant. Thank you, Aunty Bronwyn two very satisfied customers / listeners.

> **Happy is the man who finds a true friend, and far happier is he who finds that true friend in his wife.**
>
> *Franz Schubert*

59

NORMAL (1)

Aunty Bronwyn I'm at sixth form at school and one day we were discussing the topic of 'What is Normal', which had some very varied views and responses I have to say. One of the students had an MP3 of your take on Normal and wanted to play it as she said some of your views would be quite pertinent and anyway another view wouldn't go amiss. We listened to the Show and apart from being funny about your family, the show was really good. How you look at normal and quoted too from the dictionary definition on what normal is was very revealing. In fact, "normality" hasn't a real definition so there's no use trying to conform to something that doesn't exist.

It was so useful to hear because in our group we have some quite studious people and some very way out and quite gregarious if not very loud people too and both fit the definition of normal even though they are literally miles apart.

It's so easy to say he or she or they aren't normal when there's no reference to who they are and is what they do normal. In fact, is what we do normal? I know a lot of young people today are bombarded with a whole range of greedy and disingenuous media, extremely biased news coverage and persuasive advertising and it can cloud one's mind as to what it is all about.

Your very direct and down to earth approach which is definitely not politically correct is so refreshing because education is a load of controlled data and phrases thought out brought about by dull educationalists it's so uninspiring.

Also, education crams into you, facts and figures but nothing about life or additional thinking or challenging thoughts. Aunty Bronwyn you need to start targeting schools with your shows they would be lapped up. I think you have some followers here I for one. Thanks…. (Anonymous)…

How can a woman be expected to be happy with a man who insists on treating her as if she were a perfectly normal human being.

Oscar Wilde

60

NORMAL (2) DEPRESSION

Aunty Bronwyn Betty writes. Aunty Bronwyn I have been off work suffering from a bout as the doctor calls it depression. I never thought I'd be depressed like this or ever suffer from it but there we are that's what I've been diagnosed. I've always seen myself as upbeat and never dwelled upon much, always seeking the bright side of life. My mother died recently, she was very old, late 90's, so it wasn't too much of a shock and she had ill health. My cat died too, similarly she was very old in cat terms so whilst I missed her I knew that it had to happen, and it did. What really tipped the scales was a number of my friends had moved away or to homes and I realised all of a sudden, I was on my own now, and getting older, one really does need company to keep mind and soul alive and possibly body too if you can get out so much the better.

My daughter who lives far away came to visit for a few days which was very nice, she redecorated and that had a very cheering effect upon me. One evening she said she listened to a programme called "the Aunty Bronwyn Show" and that we should listen together, which I was all for. We listened, and the show was on "What's Normal" we both laughed and said that it's definitely for us. You know it was for us, because at times in your life you sometimes question yourself and think am I normal or is this normal or even are they normal and so on and you never ever get a response nor any resolution as to what is normal anyway.

Your take on being normal was excellent, I must say, and I love your family it made me smile. Your very direct approach is just so good because it is believable and so easy to take in, not a load of mumbo jumbo that leaves you feeling worse by humourless intellectual idiots. I really think you should target many senior citizens or those who like me who need time off because what you said really bucked me up. It concurred that the feelings I had were not abnormal – because we never know as no one ever says, it made me think better as my thoughts are quite acceptable – and sometimes we question them – should I be thinking this or that?

It was really a tonic even my daughter thought it excellent and phoned her husband to tell him too. Aunty Bronwyn you are my new friend now, I think of you as that, you have really cheered me up no end and I love your humour. Kind regards Betty.

Keep yourself busy if you want to avoid depression. For me, inactivity is the enemy.

Matt Lucas

61

GETTING IN WITH THE BAD CROWD TWO BLACK BOYS

Winston has written to us Aunty Bronwyn. Aunty Bronwyn academically I was good at school and to some extent within a group of black kids I was ridiculed for being brighter than them. My mum was always proud that I had done well, and I thank her now for pushing me forward when I often wanted to give up.

It's difficult as you say in your environment and when you are young you can pick up so much bad stuff. My best friend had a really bad family and spent most of his time at my house, like me he was good at school but got no support from either of his parents, at least I had my mum, in fact she used to encourage him saying 'do well and get out of this place, you can do it'.

It is easier said than done and loud mouthed negative peers make it difficult to the extent you feel so alone and have no friends. Well it happened I succumbed to "the crowd" the brainless dead and ended up in trouble with the police. It was an awful time I felt like I was going mad, didn't know what to do, where to go, frightened to go out, it was like being in an open prison but not knowing what was going to happen next. My mother was always upset but she was strong and held herself high and without her I would have really gone down, as would my friend, he really screwed up big time, but is OK now.

The police were actually quite lenient and that again was thanks to my mother and some of the teachers at school. My mother was listening to your shows and I can now understand why, although I thought they were some agony aunt stuff and that's the last thing I needed to hear, back page of a magazine but on the radio. She said one day just listen to this and it was on Choices it was great it boosted my self-esteem straight away, I subsequently listened to other programmes as did my friend, it became such a regular event as it was all the stuff I needed to hear, but where can you hear or get it from?

Aunty Bronwyn thank you so much for your shows and your funny family, they are wicked really. I think out there, there are lots of black people like myself at my age that would really benefit from listening to your shows. Thanks Aunty Bronwyn.

It is far better to be alone, than to be in bad company.

George Washington

62

HOPELESSNESS (1) RICH KID

Aunty Bronwyn Neils writes. Aunty Bronwyn I come from an intellectual and professional family who are also very cultural, and I suppose I am too in a way being the recipient of all what I have been exposed to. I am grateful in many ways as at an early age I have experienced more than most will ever do. My problem was that I didn't know what to do in life, nothing interested me at all and I was constantly "got at" from my parents and others to 'do this', 'do that', for whatever reason they made up. For them it was simple it's a job and you can probably do it and that's it.

I had made it known I didn't want to go in the family business. It was constantly "Do something until something better comes along". In theory that's fine and I really wouldn't mind doing a job in a book store or art store or something as that would be a means to an end but the constant mental challenge of "what do I really want to do" was weighing heavily upon me. It's just so easy to get into a rut and not do anything because no one ever seems to really understand you and it becomes a lonesome journey without a destination down a narrow pathway and no guide rails either, where the side drop is very steep and daunting.

Cocooned up in my bedroom doing nothing I came across your shows and just for curiosity I downloaded the programme and listened. Had I at last found someone who understood me? I heard about your life story and some of the depressing events that you had encountered and eventually overcome and the feelings that you had, I could relate to those so easily. All the topics Loneliness (that's me), Taking Control (I wasn't), Relationships (I hadn't any), Hopelessness (again me) and the rest just fitted into place.

Aunty Bronwyn it made such a difference just hearing someone who didn't know me go through all the feelings that I had and that I wasn't someone weird or strange. Even your Show on "What's Normal" made me feel quite special. As for your family it made me smile quite a few times, I think our families could be related, what a thought? I got my act together with the sole purpose of just getting any reasonably decent job just to get out of the house and get some money too. I applied for a wide range of jobs and got a few "come and have a chat with us" interviews which were very interesting.

From those I was actually offered a very junior job which I took. I've since been promoted three times and I really love it. Aunty Bronwyn you need to be made available to everyone starting out as you really put into perspective life without making it dull and without glamorising what could happen, just being real, what more can one ask. Thank you Aunty Bronwyn I owe you a G&T (or two) which I know you like (for medicinal reasons of course). All the best Neils…

63

HOPELESSNESS (2) POOR KID

Aunty Bronwyn, Ben writes. Aunty Bronwyn I come from a very working-class family, not very well educated, in fact I left school as soon as I could as I really found it hard going and it wasn't me at all. My brothers did the same. I had ambitions in life but those were dismissed in true yobbish style such "you must be joking mate – you" or "you ain't got the brains for that sort of thing" so I just kept quiet.

My girlfriend one day asked if I had any ambitions and I just told her out right that I wanted my own business and she said had I listened to your shows. I hadn't a clue who you were so said no. One evening we did listen to your show on "Taking Ownership" and you said if it is in you to do it, do it, the only thing that's stopping you is – you". You were so right, it was just my mind talk talking away with obstacles and negative thoughts fighting with what I wanted to do.

I had worked at a flower shop when I first started work but was teased and left soon afterwards, but I really enjoyed it and got on well with all the wholesalers and got to know all the flowers names and how to make bouquets and everything. You also said in your show "this is your life don't allow others to hijack it" which is just what I did earlier on. This time I thought I'm going to make this work. I got a job in a florist shop and built up my knowledge and awareness and got to know all the wholesalers again and everything to do with it.

Aunty Bronwyn I went through some very tough times, but I was so encouraged because I knew you had too, that thought kept me going. I now have six shops my family look at me totally differently, amazing how success and money talk with small minded people. Aunty Bronwyn I'm really happy although I still have more ambitious plans but it's on my terms now. If you ever want flowers on the house as a thank you, my number is on this page. When no one was listening, you were there with encouragement. All the best Ben...

Nothing prompts creativity like poverty, a feeling of hopelessness, and a bit of panic.

Catherine Tate

64

EXPECTATIONS

Philippa writes. Aunty Bronwyn I have been listening to your programmes for some time now and I have to admit that I really do look at life differently now. You are so right when you say it takes only a very small change to alter so much. Your example or analogy a small pin can burst a big balloon, or a single match can burn down a whole building fits perfectly. I was for many reasons being constantly let down or disappointed, my expectations never being met, nothing went well and then I was forever dwelling on why, why, why, why, almost to the point of becoming paranoid.

This act of regurgitating past events as you mention is a major reason as to why many people have such low self-esteem and mental health problems, never allowing themselves to blossom and not leaving the past behind. Also, whilst you are in this state of being self-absorbed you lose touch with what is actually going on around you and you become distanced between where you are in life, reality and new possibilities which hardly now exist. In short you are dwelling in a predominantly negative vacuum.

You were talking to one person on the radio and said that you thought their comment was stupid, and I took offence immediately at that because I was thinking exactly the same way as they did.

Then it all dawned upon me that in fact I was being stupid, not as a person but to myself and that anything I didn't like I tried to brush off or negate it in some way with an excuse.

I was living in a world of "all about me" and as you went on to say that if you are constantly being let down then it is you who is the common denominator nothing else.

Life hasn't singled you out, you either have lousy friends, do things which aren't that good or expect more than is reasonable, and that is just so true. Reflecting on what I was upset about there was a pattern and I was the one that allowed that pattern to continue. The final push to change momentum was listening to your show on Taking Control, I thought the time is right now to do something and what a difference it has made. Yes, I get disappointed or let down, but I move on and you know what there are always better things ahead because I can see them. Thank you, Aunty Bronwyn for just being there. All the best Philippa.

I'm not in this world to live up to your expectations and you're not in this world to live up to mine.

Bruce Lee

65

DEEP DISAPPOINTMENT

Aunty Bronwyn David writes in. Aunty Bronwyn I understand that we all get disappointed at times in life and similarly others get disappointed at us for what we may have done or not done. With me however I was bombarded by my parents at being a disappointment, not directly but they rarely gave praise and more often gave negative comments often just in passing like little quips, which really hurt if I have to be honest.

Your show on Taking Ownership made everything come alive for me in that it was myself who was allowing others to vent what they thought or felt on me and in many respects their disappointment was indeed their own selfishness and narrow mindedness not me being at default in what I had done. This change of thought and attitude almost immediately made me feel better about myself and gave me such inner strength to realise that I wasn't a disappointment at all because when I looked around me others were really pleased at what I do and want me to be friends and ask me out all of which they wouldn't do if I was that bad.

The very next time my parents made a little jibe at what I had done I just said next time do it themselves then it will be perfect. They were a little taken back but I went on to say, 'I'm fed up of you both being negative you are such a gross disappointment to me always whinging, yet you do nothing spectacular yourselves".

The advice that as you suggested in another show "turn the problem back on to itself" really worked they didn't like it one bit, but it worked. Thank you, Aunty Bronwyn everything at home has actually improved quite a lot and I'm in myself far more upfront about life. Best wished David.

We must all suffer one of two things: the pain of discipline or the pain of regret or disappointment.

Jim Rohn

66

THE COMMON DENOMINATOR – YOU

Byron writes in. Aunty Bronwyn I was at a friend's house the other day and she was listening to one of your shows. The first part was about some of your family members which actually made me laugh and I thought the rest was going to be exactly the same. Then you started talking about aspects of life and where we go wrong or can go wrong. You said something quite profound in that you were talking about relationships and how we look upon life and how they integrate and work or don't work.

My daughter has had so many boyfriends that both my wife and I are fed up of hearing the excuses of why he isn't good enough or he doesn't do this, or he doesn't do that or anything at all for that matter. It dawned upon me what you said was absolutely bang on, it was my daughter who was to blame for all her failures. She was the common element in all her failures not the other parties even if what she said was true. There must be something that is in my daughter's mind that she sees, looks for or gets wrong in seeking out a boyfriend because she has a new one nearly every week and some are really nice guys.

When I got home I told my wife about the show and we both decided to listen to the current one which we liked very much, all down to earth common sense and spoken directly which we both liked too. We got my daughter to listen to the one on relationships and I told her from the outset that the person that this is describing sounds just like you.

She didn't like what I had said but listened and afterwards made no comment, neither did we. All I did say later on was I don't want to hear anything more about your list of failed relationships, your mother and I have a life it's time you got one.

I think in hindsight my daughter took it to heart somewhat badly, anyway time passed, and things actually started to improve we heard nothing about any boyfriends whatsoever until one day she brought her current boyfriend home who she had been going out with for over six months – which in itself is a miracle. One evening she said she had listened to the show a number of times and it had actually struck a raw nerve with her.

She is totally different now even with us, her attitude has changed she's lighter in herself and with others, and more centrally focussed on enjoying life and not life trying to get life to come up to her criteria. Thank you, Aunty Bronwyn we are so pleased about the transformation of our daughter and importantly she's happier too.

67

LOVE - LIFE

Aunty Bronwyn Gisel writes in to us and says. Aunty Bronwyn. We hear a lot about love, but it is predominantly media love, it is shallow, insincere, theoretical and has no substance to it. It's just a word brandied around to make something sound good. I was listening to your Show on love and it made sense, all of it. It was just how deep love is entrenched in our lives and that the feelings of "real love" can make such a difference both to us moving forward and letting go of the past.

You mention this so many times, but you also said that with love you don't have to hold on to what is not reasonable, you don't have to suffer at the hands of others and all the negative "mind churning" that people do, and personally get depressed because they have nothing else to look forward to.

You are so right also that with love it outlaws all the negative emotions like ego, greed, hatred, anger, avariciousness, envy etc as they only get us down as we are the only ones to feel them. The anger we can hold for others no one else can take on board. Also, those who carry the past around with them and need to keep on repeating it to anyone they can talk to are very selfish and seek the past as a need for justification, whereas it means nothing to anyone else.

I think you should have courses on Love Aunty Bronwyn, because so many people really don't know what love is.

For many, love is linked to "what's in it for me" or "does this all meet my criteria if not then I don't want to know", but love is none of those things. Love can present itself in many forms and it is felt more than experienced. It is so true Aunty Bronwyn what you say about depression and loneliness and unhappiness, for so many that missing ingredient "love" has been replaced by selfishness and once that starts to rule your life you are finished, and end up living with lists of excuses and become miserable. I love your shows Aunty Bronwyn they just make me feel alive and you stand for no nonsense. Best wishes Gisel.

Time is too slow for those who wait, too swift for those who fear, too long for those who grieve, too short for those who rejoice, but for those who love, time is eternity.

Henry Van Dyke

68

LOVE – GAY

We have George write in to us. Aunty Bronwyn I'm in my early twenties and gay. I have great job, am always out and about and I suppose I'm a typical stereotype guy who likes to work hard and play hard. Most of my friends have partners, I don't, I meet many people but there is always something that just doesn't feel right or that deep connection isn't there. I'd like to think that it is not me as a person that is at fault but maybe I'm just ultra-picky?

I listened to your shows on "love" and I was fascinated because what you said all made sense. The bottom line is that we let ourselves down by having our own set of "check lists" and if others don't match it then it's bye bye. You even mentioned, that with people who have check lists subliminally cocoon themselves in their tiny little world and thus virtually no one can ever get close because there will always be just one thing that spoils the rest. You went on to say with "love", as a criterion, the real pecking order of a human being will surface, and it will not only make you see what is true and honest, but it will free yourself from your own shackles, and allow you to both harmonise with that person and share their joy.

With "love" one will feel closer and distinctive with them, want to do things with them, want to be with them, want to laugh with them, care with them, see them happy, go out of your way for them, and so on, whereas without love a degree of selfishness prevails and your "partner" is more of an acquisition rather than that special person.

What you said really made me think because I was that person who sought "points" rather than just see someone for who they were. I had to re-adjust my thoughts and try very hard to get out of that bubble that I had created and not just look for someone who was "drop dead" gorgeous but someone who was "who they were and look beyond that facade as well".

At last I found such a person and for once I was bowled over, totally different to what I had been searching for but you were so right, I don't care he's fabulous and just so nice in every way. My whole lifestyle has changed and for the better and it has given me a worth that that I've never had before. The faults that he has – and I have mine too – I just don't care about, so what, they are nothing major anyway and that's him, and I love him warts n' all.

Aunty Bronwyn I think everyone should listen to your shows on love because it makes such a difference, it's all just common sense distilled into a short show and it works. God bless you Aunty Bronwyn. Big hugs George.

> ***Being deeply loved by someone gives you strength, while loving someone deeply gives you courage.***
> *Lao Tzu*

69

LOVE - ELDERLY PENSIONER

We have a letter from Maud who writes. Aunty Bronwyn I so look forward to your shows they are a source of both amusement with your family and information, as I can relate to both. I used to have a very active life when I was younger but after my husband passed away I developed acute arthritis and it has drastically reduced my mobility. Everything what you say about love is true, I have over 40 years of marriage and three children and five grandchildren, so I can't complain.

Never the less we have to live today we can't live in our past as you so rightly say and often and that is so true. The telephone is a God send to me and I do spend a lot of time talking about a whole manner of things. I do understand why many people my age are lonely, and that is they are both set in their ways and very selfish. When it comes to phoning I'm the one that predominantly phones people, but I don't mind I get the enjoyment out of it, although I'm sure some of my colleagues would or just do sit next to the phone waiting for someone to phone them as opposed to doing it themselves. Then they wonder why they are unhappy half the time.

My family are far away some in Canada and the rest a long drive away, so frequent visits are out of the question, although they all call me and indeed when I can get the time right I phone them in Canada.

I have a number of people from the Social Services visit me and by and large they are all very good and I appreciate the short chat and often laughter too. I do have one or two neighbours who pop in and buy some bulky stuff for me, so I'm always well stocked up and I'm very thankful for that, if they see a bargain when shopping for me they buy little odds and ends and that's really nice to get a surprise or special chocolate cake now and then.

When I talk to my other friends who are close by and have the self-same people from Social Services they complain bitterly that they didn't do this or that and I often wonder what went wrong? Aunty Bronwyn you are so right. People who put out negativity received it back, their total lack of love hardened into degrees of selfishness and anger and miserableness.

I wish all these people could hear your programmes because it would do them the world of good to see that often they are the problem and not others. Keep up the good work Aunty Bronwyn, very kind wishes Maud.

> ***Your time is limited, so don't waste it living someone else's life. Don't be trapped by dogma - which is living with the results of other people's thinking. Don't let the noise of others' opinions drown out your own inner voice. And most important, have the courage to follow your heart and intuition.***
> ***Steve Jobs***

70

LOVE – COMMERCIAL

We have a letter from Brendan. Aunty Bronwyn I run a very large corporation and am jetting around all over the world. My wife enjoys a very good lifestyle and together we have seen some fabulous things and enjoyed almost the best of everything. The children are grown up and so we have a lot of time to do what we want, so much so you can fall into a scenario that you call the "all about me" syndrome.

These things happen over time and if you don't break the routine then by default you just get used to a certain style of life and want nothing less and if less appears, you by default "don't like it ahead of time" even if it is good. My wife unfortunately was taken very ill and I nearly lost her which brought everything to a head. It was a terrible time and I lost a lot of my energy and "sparkle" almost cutting off anything that didn't suit me including long-time friends. When she got better we decided to go on a cruise, but she noticed that I had changed and was a bit ratty and always complaining about people and situations and so it went on. There was a reception at work one day and a presentation and the directors wives were there and the senior managers wives too and my wife suddenly said openly to them, "do you treat everyone like that because if you do those problems in management that you were talking about may stem from you".

That really shook me but I let it ride until we got home. I said to her later that we employ the latest management techniques and run courses and have all kinds of seminars and keep an eye on what's going on etc. She retorted that management courses and anything to do with management is only as good as the way it is served and the people who implement them. If you treat people like rubbish, then the response will be equally rubbish. She said everyone responds from a little love somewhere down the line, make people feel that they are needed and worthwhile because they are as they produce a product, so show it, not robots.

On our cruise one of your shows we were listening to said, "happy workers produce better profitability and take ownership when things go wrong, happiness in the workforce comes from the top, it can't come from anywhere else". I immediately called our Personnel Team and reorganised how we looked at our staff and what they did and how we can put back something in to what they did at all levels and something sustainable not just as courses and such like which are all short-term events and fizzle out after a time.

It all worked a treat, moral has increased tremendously, and when we had to reorganise our production plants, it went far better than expected and I'm sure that is down to the fact about how we looked at the situation, as opposed to being faceless edicts just emerging from a boardroom somewhere. Best of luck Aunty Bronwyn. Brendan.

71

RESPECT (1)

We have a letter from Will. Aunty Bronwyn I love your shows many are really funny about the family and I like the way you don't mince your words. I was listening to your show on respect and it gave me so much to think about. You are absolutely right that there are two aspects to respect. One our general respect for society and those within it and the other side of the coin a respect for a person themselves. You mentioned that respect has to be earned and is not bestowed and I totally agree with you. I think far too many people think they deserve respect where deep down you have nothing but contempt for that person, although you don't often go as far as mentioning it.

Having said that, last week at a work event which was a voluntary event for a charity walk to raise money we were all discussing various ideas. One idea that I brought to the table was liked by most of the volunteers out right except for one woman who said she was offended by what I had suggested and took exception to it. I just said OK and moved on. She then said didn't you hear what I had said, so instead of getting angry I just thought what would, Aunty Bronwyn have said. So, I said I'm not in the least bit interested in what you have to say because I have no respect for you whatsoever and moved on. I'm not sure that you may have said that Aunty Bronwyn, but it worked a treat.

As you have said many times, others can only be given power or permission if you give it to them. I took it away. By the way everyone agreed with me and she eventually shut up and we went on with the meeting.

Once upon a time I would have really gotten uptight if someone had tried to "impose" themselves as if they have some divine right to their views, well they have a right to a view or opinion but that's it, and I'm so much better at getting on in life and enjoying it now.

Thank you, Aunty Bronwyn for your shows they are all "bullshit" free and it's so nice to hear the truth rather than some concocted ideology by some pseudo –intellectual who says ten words when one will do. All the best Will.

We don't need to share the same opinions as others, but we need to be respectful.

Taylor Swift

72

RESPECT (2)

Robert writes. Aunty Bronwyn your show on Respect was just spot on and you put into words quite concisely what respect is all about. It's amazing how many people seem to think because of who they are or what they do they should command respect, whereas you rightfully mentioned your respect for anyone is based upon your assessment and has nothing to do with anyone else. I agree totally that a general respect of who we are as people with regards our own safely is an unwritten agreement, thus much of the world is still a relatively safe place to go out in. But outside of our environment respect is a totally different ball game, and even prime ministers and the police have to uphold themselves for what they do otherwise respect is quickly withdrawn and unrest and often anarchy looms large.

In some societies like the Middle East there is very little respect for anything, there's a lot of unhappy subservience and fear and truth and respect are none existent. You were answering a question a while ago about parental respect and I think this was me a number of years ago. My parents weren't the best in the world and although I've done alright in life I have had to do everything myself, no safety net with my parents, they were always in it for themselves.

Even now when I occasionally contact them I always feel "why did I bother afterwards". I actually felt better from hearing your show because it lessened the guilt that I felt which I had tried to dismiss because if anything I went out of my way for my parents, but they rarely did anything of the sort for me or my sister who fortunately is happily married and cared for now.

It's a strange thing respect, sometimes it is almost thrust upon you yet at the same time it has no credentials nor is it warranted, and you really separated out what it means. Thank you, Aunty Bronwyn. Rob…

When you are content to be simply yourself and don't compare or compete, everybody will respect you.

Lao Tzu

73

PAST RESPONSIBILITIES

Aunty Bronwyn Nicole writes. I listen to your shows very often and like them very much. What I do like also is the variety of topics that you have, they are just so awesome in that they are pertinent yet are never covered anywhere else. Your show on Past Responsibilities was awesome too, I think very much as you do in many ways, just clear, concise and direct none of this pathetic politically correct stuff which is administered by substandard people to make themselves feel important. (A quote of yours also). I come from a very dysfunctional and fairly affluent family that has a lot of baggage.

Grandparents and cousins and the rest forever brining up incidents of the past and if this would have happened and if so and so hadn't done this or disgraced themselves, it's a black comedy in the making. I used to get very annoyed at all this constant clap trap but kept quiet about it so as not to make it turn into some kind of political debate which I know would have gone on and on. After hearing your show on Past Responsibilities, I thought that's it I've had enough and finished with the lot and their inane ramblings. I wasn't even born when all this supposedly devious history took place and I can't be held responsible for something which I didn't have a hand in regardless of what others think.

Just that change in my 'mind set' has made a world of difference, and I can easily dismiss what family members say and walk away, and what's more I don't care if they get upset that's for them to deal with not me.

The load has been lightened so much as I don't even feel part of the problem anymore I can see my life for what it is, and I take nothing from inheriting stories no matter what of the past.

Tomorrow is where I'm heading – which is another of your sayings, but it is so true, dancing with the past is for idiots that see no future. Thank you, Aunty Bronwyn, keep the shows coming I really look forward to hearing them. All the best Nicole.

> **As you get older, you have more responsibilities; you have more commitments, more events, kids, you're married now. You still have all the things that you've had, plus you just keep adding.**
>
> **Tom Brady**

74

LIVING IN THE PAST

Aunty Bronwyn Jeremy writes. I was introduced to your shows by a friend of mine one evening and far from it being boring which I thought it might be it was actually riveting as I had never heard anything quite like it. The show was about people who live in the past or being with those who constantly make reference to the past. This topic rang home for me as I'm surrounded by people seemingly living in the past as that is all they talk about. You are right when you say many people who live in the past use it as an excuse so as not to fail or not to make decisions always falling back on the past as an excuse as to why the future is the way it is and as we know that is all a pack of lies.

I come from a family that is steeped in the past, the past to them is almost as real as the present, and as for the future well you can't live in both at the same time, so the future is shrouded in negativity. I have broken free from all of this, in fact I refuse to listen to it which brings consternation to my family but I'm not travelling their route down memory lane which brings nothing but depressing stories that died an age ago. For many years I repeated stories of the past because I could, they were ingrained on my mind. It was all worthless but that's how you start life at times full of useless personal information that detracts from life rather than assists you, all handed down from your parents. Aunty Bronwyn you are so right it is up to us to make something of ourselves and we can't do it with repeating redundant information, that's like many politicians of today, "voices looking for somewhere to go".

Just dumping all the baggage of the past, the frequently recited stories, the incidents, everything and replace it with fresh new vibrant product that is pertinent and wholesome and has depth and breadth and something that others can relate to makes a world of difference. Just listening to your shows is therapeutic in that the mere fact that you affirm quite often what is going around in people's minds makes a world of difference. It's that connection that just sparks a feeling of "I'm not alone in how I think and feel" and it is energising and enabling and confirms to yourself that your way forward is the best for you, which is vitally important because you are you, you can't be anyone else nor they you either. Thank you, Aunty Bronwyn you really have helped me out of my rut and seen the light at last. All the best. Jeremy.

Only by going alone in silence, without baggage, can one truly get into the heart of the wilderness. All other travel is mere dust and hotels and baggage and chatter.

John Muir

75

THE PLACEBO EFFECT – ENCOURAGEMENT

Edwin writes to us. Aunty Bronwyn I listen to your shows and they have provided such encouragement for me. I know you have in the past experienced life at rock bottom so what you have to say has more meaning than all these "Self Help Theorists" who just go through the motions yet leave out the emotional aspects of what one is experiencing.

I've always been entrepreneurial in myself yet everyone around me including my family was far from that stance, they were all plodders and whilst there is nothing wrong with that no one offered any encouragement at all for anything. I know what I do is down to me it has to be and as you so frequently state too, your life is yours so don't expect anyone else to start living it because it won't happen.

The catalyst I needed came from your show Taking Charge of your life, it really did make a difference, I know it was just a few things you said but it was the fact that you said it and sometimes that's all you need a little nod in the right direction. I think we are all better than we think we are and you say that so often, we just at times need even the smallest bit of recognition from someone no matter who to believe in us, even if it's only a wish on our behalf to be successful that can get us to do big and great things.

Aunty Bronwyn your shows were always full of positive messages and you said exactly what was on your mind which also gives great confidence and you never judged a situation, allowing others to form their own conclusions. I now have a thriving business, it was not without its moments of great doubt such as "what have I got myself into" but I could hear your voice saying, "never ever give up, ever", and I didn't, and you were so right. Success is far sweeter having gone through the mill and come out the other end. I'm sure that your shows have helped many people in whatever they are seeking in life as you cover so many diverse but interesting topics.

All the best Aunty Bronwyn.. Edwin.

Sending a note of appreciation, gratitude, or encouragement can go a long way in showing someone you care.

Cynthia Germanotta

76

AN AFFAIR WITH MY FRIEND'S FATHER (1)

Aunty Bronwyn we have a letter from Sally who writes. Aunty Bronwyn My best friend and I have known each other for many years since we were at school. We have gone on holiday together and confide in each other on almost everything we do even our boyfriends.

I listened to one of your shows recently on having an affair and it was just so true what you had to say that it can be one of the most exciting things you have ever done, yet it can be so devastating afterwards with untold consequences. I would have never dreamt in a million years that I would have had an affair as I just have had, in fact it is as if I had listened to my own story but someone else telling it, I would have thought "stupid girl" you should have known better. But it wasn't someone else telling the story it was me and it is all so very real.

I was at my friends one evening and she phoned to say she wouldn't be coming home until the morning as she was a nurse and there was a massive accident nearby so extra staff were needed. Her father asked if I wanted a coffee and I said yes as I had a free evening and it just killed some time. I won't go into the details but from a coffee to an affair in two hours. I had never ever thought of my friend's father as sexy or anything else, yet it happened, and it was wonderful. The feeling I had was amazing it was like nothing I had experienced ever before in every sense of the word.

I really felt guilty afterwards not about what had happened but the fact that I could never share this with my friend and from now on I would have this dark secret every time I was with her that I wouldn't be able to share. This affair went on for about six months as and when the situation permitted. The fact that it then started to become too familiar became a little scary. Aunty Bronwyn you were so right with what you said about affairs and the fact that when they start all your "logic buttons" get switched off, and the "I'm an adult doing adult things" overrides everything, although those buttons soon turn quickly back on afterwards.

Your advice was greatly taken in, I knew that the affair couldn't continue, and I had to change my thoughts, stance, ideology, what I did, for if I didn't I would be just walking around with guilt, depression, anxiety and lack of self-worth about myself, and I really don't think I'm a bad person.

I also didn't want to distance myself from my friend either but not to keep looking at her and thinking "I've had an affair with your dad", which would be awful. As you also mentioned when you have an "affair" as opposed to a "relationship" everything is somewhat clandestine and that poses enormous problems usually for little final reward. This was so true, it did start to get me down, but you said very strongly "don't go down that route" respect yourself even if you are full or regret, the past is where it now lies, and the future is where you are going and where everything else lies. Guilt has no purpose in life as it is a past event and only hinders progress, what has been done has been done good or bad or anything in-between.

It is all over now, I do actually feel better and a million times the wiser about life and what can happen. Thank you, Aunty Bronwyn for just being there with your thoughts on the subject, and importantly how best to get over it all and start afresh. God bless you Aunty Bronwyn…

77

AN AFFAIR WITH MY FRIEND'S FATHER (2)

Aunty Bronwyn Derick writes with a letter similar to our previous one. Aunty Bronwyn life can throw some real weird blows to you at times, completely out of the blue and totally unexpected. My best mate's sister was getting married and I had been invited to the wedding. I have known them both since primary school, so I was almost a part of their family as he was in my own. The wedding was quite away away, and so we were staying overnight in the hotel of the reception, I was sharing with my mate. We are both gay and both our parents know but are just friends nothing more. Because of logistics my mate went with his mum to the reception in her car early on and because I worked later as did his dad I was to go with him a little later in his car.

I arrived at my mate's home and his dad had just got in. He said he was just going to have a shower and a cup of tea then we'd be off. I said I'd make the tea, so his dad went for his shower. I was making the tea and his dad came into the kitchen in a towel looking for some socks, which were in a big laundry basket. He noticed that I was staring at him because he had an amazing body. I knew he was sporty but nothing more than that. I said you've got a great body and actually started to feel a bit horny. He got his tea and we chatted and I think he could see me getting a bit hot and my eyes were shifting all over the place.

Anyway, we never finished the tea needless to say we were a little late arriving that evening. I had had a penchant for older guys, but my mate's dad never crossed my mind. We had a few encounters after that which I had to admit were good but the deception that it took to make everything work out and the fact that it was my mate's dad was all a bit too much.

I heard your programme Aunty Bronwyn on Having an Affair and you were spot on with what happens and how you feel. It was actually quite good to hear it all as I feel better about it now and about myself. If I hadn't heard your show I think it would have been something that I would have had on my mind all the time and not being able to come to terms with it. I daren't tell my mate and think it is all best forgotten if you can ever do that. I'd just like to say when something like this happens you have no reference point to check in with, it is as it is. But thankfully your show really helped me, and all is good again. Thank you, Aunty Bronwyn.

Reality is easy. It's deception that's the hard work.

Lauryn Hill

78

MIDDLE AGED WIFE CRISIS

Aunty Bronwyn Steve has written in. Aunty Bronwyn I have my own little business and my wife works part time at the local educational trust. Life is OK I suppose in that it suites us, neither of us are big at going out so homely comforts are our thing. We are both just over 50 and I think we have gotten into a very staid way of life.

I have had a few health issues of recent date and I've noticed my wife has put on a lot of weight and looks very large. We were talking the other night about life and the issues that we are facing and things we would like to do or accomplish or like to happen in a general conversation. My wife mentioned that she has indeed lost interest in doing just about anything. She likes her work and she also goes to a Charity evening once a week which she enjoys but outside of that nothing, just watch TV from the moment she gets in until bedtime.

My wife's sister said one day to listen to Aunty Bronwyn for no other reason that she liked it and the bits of humour too and she thought we would. Well we did listen to your Shows and they were very interesting I think I can say we both look forward to hearing them. The Show on taking ownership and relationships was very informative. It's just the fact that what you said make complete sense and put into perspective our lives, whatever they happen to be for us.

What we both like and how we enjoy our lives are our business no matter what it happens to be. It was to some extent an affirmation that with a few odd bits and pieces here and there our lives are fine for us. I think my wife had had thoughts that she had lost much of what she should be as a wife, but your show quickly put that back to where it should be that she is fine just the way she is. This has made her want to lose weight and now goes to a slimming club and loves being with others in the same boat it has brought a new lease of life to her.

Thank you, Aunty Bronwyn, so often it's just hearing a few choice words at the right time which we all need from time to time to make a world of difference. Thanks again, Steve.

You will never be happy if you continue to search for what happiness consists of. You will never live if you are looking for the meaning of life.

Albert Camus

79

DAUGHTER AND PARENTS DOMINEERING IN OLD AGE

Aunty Bronwyn we have a letter from Mel he writes. Aunty Bronwyn my wife's parents live not far from us we live in a small town. Up until now it has been OK in that my wife visited them for short bursts and gets some shopping for them or at times medication, so far, all OK. However now they are both getting less mobile and expect my wife to be a taxi service for them ringing her up at work or at home as when they want something. She feels guilty about them not be able to help themselves, but in all honesty, they never have helped themselves ever, always putting on others and expecting them to run around them.

I need the car at times for my business and have put my foot down saying I need it and I don't care what your parents want, if we weren't here they would have to make alternative arrangement I'm not having them selfishly interrupt our lives as an on-call taxi service when they feel like it, parents or not. My wife took this in good stead but never the less wanted to help out, which I can understand too.

We listened to your shows Aunty Bronwyn about taking ownership, relationships, parents, and a number of others and it really distilled that no matter who you are or what your circumstances you don't have to be a 'lapdog' for anyone. When people take you for granted then that's the time to act and as you said that I realised that I needed to nip this all in the bud now before it got too far out of hand.

I went up to see my wife's parents, who are quite nice actually and told them straight the situation, which they didn't like, but never the less it had to be said. I didn't want my wife being constantly on edge just waiting for the next thoughtless command and blackmail call asking her to do this or that.

It worked, a bit of coercing on my part but it worked. Thank you, Aunty Bronwyn for just having those programmes, sometimes you know what to do but just need to hear it to get yourself to do it. Thank you and we love your shows. All the best Mel.

Sometimes you have to be selfish to be selfless.

*** Edward Albert***

80

WHEN RELIGION CAN TAKE OVER

Aunty Bronwyn Kevin writes. I've always been religious, brought up that way and it has, to be honest in my belief helped me over a few bad patches in my life. I met a few people who I thought were very nice, religious people some time ago and I was invited to their Church. I went, and I thoroughly enjoyed it, it was as if that was the missing piece in my life. I got involved in all sorts of activities and met new people and suddenly I had a really busy social life.

I can understand at times that religion or indeed anything can suddenly overtake your life, and this did. I needed to put God into perspective and there is a difference between been an active Christian and become obsessed with it to the point that you lose your element of humanity which is in fact Anti-Christian in itself. The last thing I wanted was to be a bigot and judgemental and biased to the extreme and start taking sides and so it all goes on.

I listened to your show on God and Religion and it was fascinating in that it really put into perspective Religion and God and the difference between, and how as individuals we live our lives. That was an eye opener for me because it was far from being biased it was as it really is, and respected whatever view you take, but it interjected a reality within it all. It has changed my views and indeed I'm even a better and happier Christian now that I was before because my journey and pathway is between me and God and no one else, ever.

Thank you, Aunty Bronwyn, I'm getting a few of my colleagues to listen to your shows. God bless. Kevin.

81

HAPPINESS – WHY AREN'T I HAPPY

Aunty Bronwyn Zadvika writes to us and says. Aunty Bronwyn I've been in the UK now for about 6 years and I like it very much. I am originally from Poland where my family live. I used to speak English in my job in Poland so coming to the UK wasn't a big deal with regards language and getting on with people.

I was lucky to get a good job shortly after I arrived, and it not only paid well but I got trips back home for business too, so all was well for me. Initially I met a number of people where I worked and where I lived which was very nice and they were very nice too. After a time, you like to find certain people who are on your wavelength and mean something just a little more. I found it difficult finding a boyfriend although I had many male friends some Polish too but nothing that I would like to take further than friendship.

A friend of mine who is also Polish introduced me one evening to your shows and I was impressed by what you had to say on many subjects. One evening your topic was Happiness and although I wasn't unhappy I wasn't that happy either. Aunty Bronwyn you are so right in what you say about happiness. It is not always easy to absorb the truth, but the truth is the truth, regardless of what you want to think or what excuses you make to hide the reality.

Happiness was within me all the time and this perpetual looking and analysing and searching was just me evading what real happiness was because I had a set idea about happiness and it never coincided with what the real happiness was all around me. It's strange just looking at something from a different perspective can make all the difference. It has made a difference Aunty Bronwyn, thank you so much. Zadviga.

> *I just find myself happy with the simple things. Appreciating the blessings God gave me.*
>
> **DMX**

82

LONELINESS

Aunty Bronwyn Racheal has written to us. Aunty Bronwyn I listened to your show the other week on Loneliness. It is something I can associate with if I'm honest but not admit to. You were right on a number of points in that you don't have to be on your own to be lonely and that one of the biggest causes of loneliness is in fact selfishness.

I've always been a bit of a loner even though I've had friends or acquaintances around me. I would call acquaintances friends as a generic title, but I don't think I've ever had a close friend or someone I could mess around with and do silly things without being embarrassed or even confide in. You really made me feel uncomfortable when you described how many lonely people are, how they are usually the last to volunteer things, or the first in the queue if anything is going free, or that the expression "I keep to myself" meaning don't do anything for me because I don't want to reciprocate. Life is on a perpetual check list and yes you do subliminally keep financial accounts of who does what and who phoned whom and the list goes on. To be honest is there any wonder why you are lonely.

Your list went on but that was enough for me to have a fit of remorse. Your other shows such as Taking Charge or Ownership left me no option at last than to change my life.

I can't get older and older and just expect all of a sudden for it to change when I do nothing to contribute to it. It's not that I don't have the money to make a difference.

I've made a difference Aunty Bronwyn and even a number of my friends have commented on a change in me and even asked me to events of their other friends, something that would have never happened before. I've stopped making mental lists and it has worked a treat. I've even got myself a boyfriend and offered to take him out to dinner not knowing he was quite wealthy. He found it very endearing and said rarely does anyone ask him out because they know he's wealthy. I'm loving life Aunty Bronwyn thank you so, so, so, so much. Big hug Racheal.

> *I was quiet, a loner. I was one of those children where, if you put me in a room and gave me some crayons and a pencils, you wouldn't hear from me for nine straight hours. And I was always drawing racing cars and rockets and spaceships and planes, things that were very fast that would take me away.*
>
> *Gary Oldman*

83

FAILURE – NOT AS BAD AS YOU THINK

Aunty Bronwyn Eyal writes to us. Aunty Bronwyn I must say that I was so energised by your show on Failure. For years things had not gone right for me, I wasn't in a bad state but mentally I was feeling low and every day I had to almost psych myself up to start it with a cheerful attitude.

I've tried a whole load of things and none of them have gone well despite putting 110% into them. I started comparing what others did and they just seemed to glide to success, although I know they had trying times it all came out well. My stuff just 'put putted' out and that was it. Your Show on "Taking Charge of your life" was also a turning point when you said, "never give up, ever, ever, ever, despite what happens never ever give up". The result will be so much sweeter, it's your life, do it for you. I just needed to hear that Aunty Bronwyn, nothing more, just someone like you who has been there experienced life at both sides of the coin, it makes so much difference.

I pursued my business aim starting a small but specialist fragrance business, and despite endless setbacks it still excited me so with you whispering in my mind, "Don't give up" I continued, despite more setbacks I continued.

Then it happened, as you also say, it only takes a small pin to burst a big balloon, and similarly one contact changed my entire working situation, from struggling to very viable almost overnight.

AGONY LETTERS

You are so right, it is so sweet the reward of success and I really feel I have achieved something and am proud of myself. My life has changed dramatically, and it just remains to say a massive thank you, and please, please let me know what kind of perfume you like, and it will be in the post by return. Thank you, Aunty Bronwyn, big big hug Eyal.

I can accept failure, everyone fails at something. But I can't accept not trying.

Michael Jordan

84

POLITICAL CORRECTNESS

Andre has written to us. Aunty Bronwyn I work in the local council, I have a good job and I like it very much as I get to move around the Borough a lot, meet many people and it is always interesting. What is endemic in places like councils and government offices is the bureaucracy which seems to go hand in hand with it all and now this Political Correctness which drives me mad, as I know it does you too.

A number of incidents have arisen where the Politically Correct card has been played to gain advantage, by the usual selfish small-minded people that see life one way and one way only. This was wearing a bit thin because the vast majority were happy with the overall stance that was being taken, just the few regular whingers that know no better that are an embarrassment in life. I loved your show on Political Correctness and if you ever stood to be a politician you'd have my vote.

Your hints and tips on what you do when confronted by such low life people is very simple and direct and that is to take away their assumed authority, that is because they say they don't like something they then think everyone has to bow down to them, well, that's just not so. My change of attitude has made a world of difference and as you said on another of your shows "turn the situation back on to itself" and that really does make a difference big time.

Even in the council where people go around talking to each other about other people and situations as if it is of world importance just shows you the small-minded quality of them, although some of it is fostered.

Maybe this is a small thing Aunty Bronwyn, and it really niggled me, but now I feel so much different and have a far better standing with myself and can help others far better too by putting these little nobodies back where they should have been in the first place. Thank you, Aunty Bronwyn. Andre.

> ***Every adversity, every failure, every heartache carries with it the seed of an equal or greater benefit.***
>
> ***Napoleon Hill***

85

ANGER – SERVING NO PURPOSE

Poppy writes to us. Aunty Bronwyn I come from a family that seems to run on anger, they are always getting at each other or someone or something as if they don't life doesn't have any meaning. They always feel they need to assert their point of view which often with angry people is embarrassingly wrong in many ways. It was at times for me getting me down, I tended to walk away and not enter into the affray even if at I did generally agree with what they had to say occasionally.

I love listening to your shows they are so varied and often allow me into an area of life that's really new and at times a bit "full on" but in a good way. Then I heard your show on Anger and that really put into perspective what I had been privy to for such a long time. All those shouting matches and as you called them "failed Hollywood drama scenes" that were fabricated for effect, yes it does say so much about how low they are mentally as people to have to do this to justify themselves.

It is amazing how easy it is when you are in the know as to how to deal with others and how you can see that time after time they fall into their staid, dull boring tired routines and haven't moved on in life. It's repetition from the same old record. I've have moved on light years now in one fell swoop, I just don't allow what they or anyone says to get to me, why should I? I feel better more confident and my ability to cope which was OK before is even better now. Thank you, Aunty Bronwyn for your lovely shows. All the best Poppy.

86

MY SECRET WORLD (1)
WHAT'S YOUR FETISH?

Aunty Bronwyn Clive writes to us. Aunty Bronwyn what a revelation to hear your show on "My Secret World". This kind of programme doesn't exist anywhere else and the way you talk about it all free from judgment or a panel of pseudo "know all's" that know nothing is amazing.

I'm a cross dresser, I'm married have two grown up children, excellent job and my wife knows all about me. I have had this fetish for many years now and go away for the odd weekend to be "my alternative self" with others of similar inclinations. The public get a kick out of hearing about such practises as they think it kinky and yet know nothing about it or of the type of people who are involved, as if they don't have any weird habits too. They also feel that it is a gay thing, yet I've never had an affair with another man ever nor do I want to. In reality it is no different from "train spotting" or "motor cross" or anything else, it's just what floats your boat and in reality, as you put it so bluntly, "It's no one else's business whatsoever".

The show was amazing in that it touched on a number of different "fetishes" that everyday people have, and as you said very early on in the show the only reason that people get surprised is because of their own ignorance, prejudices or narrow mindedness, sometimes they can't even explain themselves.

AUNTY BRONWYN SPEAKING TO JOHN RUSHTON

I don't have a problem with what I do although I know many who do as it is a very secret world. I'm sure your show will have helped many people enjoy their lives better and I have recommended a number to listen to it. I like all the shows Aunty Bronwyn, but you surpassed yourself with this one. Excellent thank you so much. Clive.

> *The beloved is the ultimate fetish.*
>
> **Mason Cooley**

87

MY SECRET WORLD (2)
BONDAGE AND THE REST

Aunty Bronwyn Charles has written to us. I was taken back Aunty Bronwyn on your show on Fetishes, as apart from the odd documentary very little if anything is ever mentioned about what people get up to. If anything, it is all an "expose" of what some media journalist seems to have unravelled even though it's nothing new and requires no input from anyone else. Your comments were, I can say breath taking as you offer no judgment whatsoever and I know you have experienced life to the full so to you, life is what it is. To others life is what little they know and no more, which sadly depicts their life.

I'm into bondage and being domineered and humiliated I love being told what to do, dress up in a collar and be spanked. I have an excellent job in the City. If you have never experienced something that really turns you on – whatever it is – then refrain from comment. I frequent private parties and events where this takes place and it is a very closely guarded circle, quite a number of prominent people are seen there enjoying a freedom they cannot get anywhere else.

Your comments on people and life are so refreshingly direct, not rude but direct and you don't take any flak from anyone. What I think is very productive is that 'out there' there must be thousands of people who have some sort of harmless fetish and can't correspond or daren't correspond with anyone so just live with pent up emotions.

I do hope many people listened to your show as it I think it will give so much hope and comfort and enable them to live better and more rewarding lives.

Thank you, Aunty Bronwyn for this show I even felt better myself from just listening to it. If you ever feel you would like to join us let me know!!!! All the best Charles.

I love clothes. I can't control myself. I have a huge fetish for shoes and clothes and make-up. I'm the kind of person who doesn't like to wear things over and over again.

Hilary Duff

88

ON THE GAME

Aunty Bronwyn Julia writes. Aunty Bronwyn I was listening to your show last night on "On the Game" and it was just so interesting, you really did get to grips with the emotions of why people do it, the different types of people who do it, and even those women who do it secretly who are housewives and earn a lot of money. You also touched on the "forced trade" which is a different ball game altogether.

I got into selling myself through desperation. The situation to make some cash just presented itself and I took the opportunity, it wasn't that difficult, although I know for many women psychologically it would be stepping over the line big time, but for me it wasn't. From my experience most of the girls are quite nice people although there are all types and all levels, but then that goes for life anyway, wealthy people and banks ripping money off ordinary wage earners happens every day and nothing is done about it.

It is strange to say Aunty Bronwyn, but it was just so nice to hear you talk about the "profession" as you did. You made no moral comment only of the potential welfare or lack of it and that the profession exists like it or not and it exists around the world in every country. You did touch on the future for many people and this is always the big question, how long can you keep on doing this. I liked the show Aunty Bronwyn it made a great difference and put real issues and potential possibilities into a doable situation which at some stage and is worthy of thought.

Thank you Aunty Bronwyn I have real respect for you and your comments, people like me rarely get anything to help them in life, it's just so nice to have someone not poke fun or ridicule or dramatis what we do. All the best. Julia.

***Software is like sex:
it's better when it's free.***

Linus Torvalds

89

YOU'VE GOT TO BE IN IT TO WIN IT

Paul writes to us Aunty Bronwyn. It's so easy to get into a rut over time that you start to talk as if with experience about things which you never participate in. On your show "You've Got To Be In It To Win It" it is so true. The amount of people who say "I'm not lucky" or "that never happens to me" never do anything so of course nothing happens. I used to be like that, after your show I bought a Lottery ticket and dismissed it, yet I won £10. I've won nothing since, but it did open up that the possibility exists and that if I enter anything I stand a chance.

Your show "Taking Ownership" also changed my train of thought, as did "The Only Thing Stopping you is You". These are so true statements, yet on your own at times you start thinking too much about a whole array of things, and it then becomes tangled in your mind, and then you lose the thread and then that goes elsewhere and before you know it you have talked yourself out of it. You then only need one negative comment and that's it you're finished.

Aunty Bronwyn just one of your very positive and upbeat shows washed away every little bit of negativity, why can't there be more people like you around. You are so right too that we must only mix with positively minded people the rest have no place in our lives no matter who they are. Thank you, Aunty Bronwyn keep up the fabulous shows. Cheers. Paul.

90

THE FEELING TO BE NEEDED

Angela writes to us Aunty Bronwyn. Aunty Bronwyn, I loved your show "The Feeling to Be Needed" it was just what I needed big time. It's amazing how many people go around in their lives with nothing and no one in particular. Yes, everyone may have friends or acquaintances but not that special person which doesn't have to be a partner, just that certain someone who thinks of you and you of them.

It is so important to want to be needed by that certain person no matter who they are for if you are not cared for or loved, life can be so shallow and that's when mental health problems develop, and loneliness starts to creep into to staid negative routines, and selfishness takes a hold because the mind thinks of only one thing, me, me me, as you rightly say. Once you become insular you by default lock out others, and then become complacent, and then you lose the ability and everything else thereafter becomes a chore and after that you become hopeless.

Aunty Bronwyn this was all me, what you described was in fact me deteriorating because of myself, nothing more nothing less. A person full of self excuses and a creeping laziness and lethargy all because I was going downhill and no one cared for me, and why should they when I cared for no one but myself.

Your show literally pulled me back from that brink Aunty Bronwyn, it gave me another chance and I'm just so glad I took that opportunity as I actually have a boyfriend now, and I'm so thrilled.

I really hope others listen to your shows Aunty Bronwyn because I'm sure it will have the exact same effect and it changes your life in an instant. Thank you, Aunty Bronwyn. God bless you. Angela.

> ***What I needed most was to love and to be loved, eager to be caught. Happily I wrapped those painful bonds around me; and sure enough, I would be lashed with the red-hot pokers or jealousy, by suspicions and fear, by burst of anger and quarrels.***
>
> ***Saint Augustine***

91

LETTING GO

Aunty Bronwyn Felix writes to us. Aunty Bronwyn I come from a quite possessive family, I don't know why but everyone keeps a hold of what they have got and I suppose it has rubbed off. For me however it went further than that I just seemed to feel that I needed to know about everything and everyone because if I didn't then life would run ahead of me, and then I don't know what would happen. The truth, as you mentioned in your show "Letting Go" is a million miles away from the need to hold on to superfluous information. We in reality need to know very little because the vast array of knowledge whether it is interesting or not is outside of both our control and has little ultimate effect. Being nosey is an illness in itself.

I was for many years the holder of masses of information not knowledge just information that had little to do with me, and when you do that you need constant updates, just like watching a TV soap, all made up. My life even suffered because I was forever updating stuff and then worrying what would happen if this didn't work or that didn't work, and the very worst thing about following others is it negates who you are. After your broadcast I just stopped literally following anyone and everything, concentrating on what I wanted and all of a sudden, to have a life again. Everything else I lost interest in, and I was able to think more clearly and concisely too and develop what I wanted from life.

I stopped following all the celebrity rubbish, predominantly silly people made famous many of whom were constantly in rehab and I used to read about that as if it was important news, who cares? If you don't respect yourself and place importance on yourself as you say Aunty Bronwyn, then there is little hope of anything good ever happening, and you get hurt just so much easier. That's all changed now thank goodness.

Aunty Bronwyn thank you for your shows they are such an inspiration and this one in particular just rang the right sound for me. I'm sure many people have benefited from your shows in whatever way is pertinent to themselves. And I also love your family, it always makes me smile. All the best Felix.

> ***The point of human evolution is adapting to circumstance. Not letting go of the old, but adapting it, is necessary.***
>
> ***Sonali Bendre***

92

THE FUTURE IS WHAT YOU MAKE IT

Mike has written in to us Aunty Bronwyn. Aunty Bronwyn I was really taken back by what you had to say about the future. It's not that it was mind breaking or anything but the fact that I think possibly like many people they thought that what the future has in store was and somehow is inevitable. I actually have to agree with you that the future is a time and a space and how we direct our lives is a decisive action that can deliver where we are to a large extent in the future.

Everything points to what you have to say is true, if we don't save we don't have, if we don't look after ourselves we won't be so good and so it goes on. We have to be decisive otherwise life will take us by default and then if we end up where we didn't want to go or be then it is to a large extent down to us that that happened. I like your shows Aunty Bronwyn they very often challenge my thinking, but I have to admit to myself later that what you had said has some value-added credence to it and I usually come around to thinking that way.

It has by default changed my thoughts about my life and I look a little more carefully now especially at long term goals or desires and try to keep them on a common road in trying to reach them. I know many things outside of our control can change our direction dramatically but at the same time I feel more comfortable now in steering myself forward with some definition and hopefully to a better place. Thank you, Aunty Bronwyn for your shows one of the best there is on the airways. All the best. Mike..

93

CHANGING LIFE – MID TERM

Aunty Bronwyn Lew writes to us. Aunty Bronwyn I hold down a very good job, but it was getting to me. I was suffering all sorts of minor conditions and feelings and those" mind gremlins" as you speak about were waging a war in my mind. I was starting to lose the plot and I knew it, I had seen others in similar situations and age almost overnight crumble because they couldn't let go of the salary / lifestyle.

Your shows on 'Taking Ownership' and 'Making the Change Work' really got me thinking in that the only one who can change my life is me or I could just wait until I collapse and then it happens for you by default. It's not easy in mid-life making a career change especially today, but I went ahead and put my c.v. out there and contacted endless recruitment agencies which is a soulless task and put feelers around too, you just do what you can. What came back wasn't very enlightening but the process as you mentioned isn't about just making a change in career it is changing your mind set too and that can be the most difficult thing. Then I remembered what you said in that what were my likes and dislikes in life and you know I never entered those into the equation at all. All I had done to date was re-state what I had been doing and the positive points but not what I as a person really liked. So, I re-did my c.v. based upon what I liked in life and expected and sent them off, expecting either nothing to happen or very low salaried positions to come back, but nothing ventured etc.

It's amazing that self-ignorance often holds you back, whereas you often state Aunty Bronwyn just go for it, what's the worst that can happen – nothing. What's the best that can happen –

something. Well after a while things did start to move and I'm in a job I really love now, I feel better more refreshed and alive with no daily dread or heavy pressures. Thank you, Aunty Bronwyn for just saying what was the obvious but you know sometimes you have to hear it from someone else for it to register. I'm sure your shows have helped many more people. Best Lew.

To improve is to change; to be perfect is to change often.

Winston Churchill

94

I'M IN NEED OF LOVE

Aunty Bronwyn Ellen writes in. Aunty Bronwyn I love your shows they are just so different and down to earth, I really feel uplifted after hearing other people write in, often having endured terrible things in their lives and overcome their difficulties. I listen to all their stories and I think my problems are nothing compared to those I've just heard, in fact I feel a little guilty at what I seem to think is important. Do I rectify my situation? You often say, "do nothing and nothing will happen" and that was me.

I have friends Aunty Bronwyn, but I really needed some love, something more special than just someone to meet for a drink or coffee or a late-night phone chat. I was listening to your shows on Love, and if I have to be honest I do have love all around me, it may not be the Hollywood version with glitter, but I do have love there already, it's just that I wanted it my way and not the way it is. You do have a knack of identifying what's what Aunty Bronwyn, and I really appreciate what you say because it is the truth, not just smart empty words.

If I look back over the years at what my friends have done and I haven't done because I really didn't appreciate fully their involvement in my life I could be quite upset. I thought right, it's time I reciprocated, but in a genuine way not just buy something out of the blue for them because that would be so transient I wanted to make a difference to their lives. Bit by bit I offered help, to do things, go off for days, see things and it has made a world of difference not only to how I feel but the quality of my life and my relationship with just about everyone around me.

Aunty Bronwyn, thank you for getting me to open my eyes, I was wallowing in the "poor old me syndrome" another of your sayings for so long I couldn't see the love around me. Thank you so much for your shows life is so much better now. Kind wishes Ellen.

Immature love says: 'I love you because I need you.' Mature love says 'I need you because I love you.'

Erich Fromm

95

BEING REJECTED AND TURNED DOWN

Ronaldo writes to us Aunty Bronwyn. Aunty Bronwyn I know none of us like to get turned down it just goes against the grain with how we feel. It seemed recently that everything I applied for, requested, sent off for was fraught with problems or denials or what was asked of me made it not worthwhile, I was beginning to get really down and feel low. I then came across your show on "Rejection" and I had to listen to it. I knew it wouldn't change anything that I did but I had to hear what you had to say.

I was so wrong, and I could even hear you scolding me in my mind in a nice way saying, 'there's nothing worse than a closed mind to stop the free flow of things happening', which is so true. You say absolutely nothing that is negative Aunty Bronwyn and you are right to do so because we do create our own reality and if we are negative then so is our reality.

You mentioned that if you get turned down ten times or a hundred times, so what, keep on going. Those scientists that fail every day for years on end trying to discover cures etc do so with a good heart and purpose. Those that give up fail, those that never give up never fail, it's that simple. You place yourself on a level of your own choosing. It's OK to get a little "down" but then you get up and off you go again.

I can hear every word you say. Everyone who succeeds never gives up and often in the process of carrying on one actually finds something far better that you never knew about.

My spell of being rejected has seemingly come to an end in as much as a number of things I applied for and sent off for have all come back positive. Like busses they all come at once. Thank you, Aunty Bronwyn for your advice it really cheered me up at a time I wanted a positive voice to give me that push to go on. It's so true that at times all we want is that little pat on the back that we are OK, and things will get better and then the rest falls into place. Thank you, Aunty Bronwyn big hugs Ronaldo.

We all learn lessons in life. Some stick, some don't. I have always learned more from rejection and failure than from acceptance and success.

Henry Rollins

96

COPING WITH DIFFICULT PEOPLE

Neil writes to us Aunty Bronwyn. Aunty Bronwyn I have a very difficult elderly mother, I have very difficult people at work and I have a new set of neighbours who I also find difficult not like the previous ones at all. Over time this has become very depressing not from a physical aspect but just negativity, negativity, negativity everywhere I go there seems to be no respite it's just this perpetual darkness and no light. The result of all of this was that I was becoming very short tempered or just ignored people which didn't help the situation in any way.

I heard your show on 'Coping with Difficult People' and it highlighted some very simple self- options. You also mentioned that you were subliminally allowing this negativity to get to yourself and in one of tour shows you said if things don't go well with others "turn the situation back upon itself". Why should you be the recipient of others negativity, assuming you aren't the cause yourself and I was sure I wasn't. Instead of just reacting or becoming glum or moody or whatever I just carry on with my life as I want to. With my mother I just turned around and said if you can't be nice then get someone else to help you because I've had enough of your selfishness. It was a shock for me to say that and it was certainly a shock to her to hear it, but I persevered and ignored her until she was desperate for help – it wasn't desperate in a life-threatening sense, and then what a transformation. From resident dragon to purring cat in seconds.

As for the neighbours I smile say hello and smile again, it freaks them out but it's working they are saying hello. Those at work similar treatment, it works too.

Aunty Bronwyn you are so right when it comes to dealing with others, there's always an agenda towards ill manners and ignorance, always, but it is not your agenda so don't accept it. Never go down to their level and above all never ever allow your ego to raise its head, that's the kiss of death in an instant. None of this is rocket science as you put it Aunty Bronwyn but sometimes we get locked into a narrow little world of our own then start playing the game with them. If they do this I'll do that, etc, whereas doing nothing is very often the best route forward.

For me Aunty Bronwyn lesson learned, I hope it works for others because the route I followed doesn't leave a negative trail and I have nothing to keep up with or add to or raise the bar to meet, nothing, it's just me doing what I like doing which is all very great. Thank you, Aunty Bronwyn you have come out trumps yet again. Best Neil…

All things are difficult before they are easy.

Thomas Fuller

97

CREATIVE FRUSTRATION

Aunty Bronwyn Paula writes to us. Aunty Bronwyn, I'm weird I have to say that to start with, not that I think I'm weird but everyone else does. My hair is 1001 different colours and I make most of my own clothes. My hero amongst many is Vivien Westwood as she makes designer attire out of the most unusual or unlikely things and I like that a lot. The trouble is that I live in the sticks miles away from anywhere and where everyone around me doesn't even have a collective brain cell between them. I'm not sure what they really think of me, but my mum has stopped saying anything and my father pretends it doesn't happen as he just can't get his head around any of it. He wore a red carnation at a wedding recently and he thought he was verging on being a reprobate. I still don't think he's gotten over it.

I love your Broadcasts Aunty Bronwyn, as you just say and do as you feel and if others don't like it fine, I love that. Why should you be put down by those who are lesser people. It's hard going where I am as I seem to be my own audience as to what I do, although I provide a talking point wherever I go in my locality. I'm sure everyone thinks I'm drugged up and spend days in wild orgies, whereas its cups of tea in my bedroom creating my clothes. I listened to your broadcast on Creative Frustration and thought could you read my mind Aunty Bronwyn, because it was me you were talking about. Everything you said was about me and what I have to put up with or the snide comments I get, and the great frustration of not being able to talk to any like-minded people.

What you had to say gave me great strength about myself about being proud of who I am, about keeping for now anyway my own council, for upholding my own values about being creative, about not giving in to morons who can't tell the difference between black and white, about seeing a vision of where I want to go whereas others see nothing but their nose end. About weathering the storm and I loved what you said about those who "go with the flow". That the two main things that go with the flow are dead fish and used toilet paper, I really had to smile at that.

Than you Aunty Bronwyn for your words, they made such a difference to my self-esteem, and indeed to me smiling through it all until I make the next move into designing my clothes or working in design at some creative company. Big hug Aunty Bronwyn lots of love Paula...

> ***Our fatigue is often caused not by work, but by worry, frustration and resentment.***
>
> **Dale Carnegie**

98

DON'T WASTE TIME ON INSIGNIFICANT PEOPLE

Aunty Bronwyn Emmanuel writes. Aunty Bronwyn it's difficult at times in life to move forward because sometimes you are not sure what to do and at other times it is just not practical to do what you want for many reasons. I really did enjoy your show on "Don't Waste Time on Insignificant People" because as I've found out there are a lot of them around. Everyone is an expert or has an opinion until something goes wrong and then you just can't see any of them around, such is their real lack of personal strength.

When you are in a bit of a quandary in life you tend to listen to anybody really just in case they have a glimmer of hope or a flicker of information that you could take hold of or work on or anything that may help you move forward. Most people have some experience on something or another, yet it rarely is what you like or want to do, or if it is it's not conducive to how you would do it in your circumstances in your situation at this present time. As you rightly say the things called "time lines" come into play and that changes just about everything even parallel identities or scenarios.

I think I had my fill of "know all's" and your show definitely outlined what I had just been going through and experiencing.

As you pointed out Aunty Bronwyn, sometimes you can get into a rut of asking others just for the mere fact that it could be possible that there is an answer there awaiting you, but on the other hand you could spend the rest of your life waiting for those odds to fall into your favour. I needed to hear this Aunty Bronwyn, because I know you would say just as it is and not from any personal motive or ego or anything else. Regardless of others I've made my decisions based upon what I know and I'm actually doing better than I thought, I can see and feel what is right within even if a little nervous at times, it's me doing it for me and I feel so good.

Thank you Aunty Bronwyn I really owe you a G&T, which I know you say you have to force down to be sociable, as do I frequently!! All the best Emmanuel.

Time is what we want most, but what we use worst.

William Penn

99

NO SEX RELATIONSHIP

Aunty Bronwyn Margery has written to us. Aunty Bronwyn you have some really eclectic topics on your shows and I love them all. Many are never ever discussed elsewhere and if they are there is always a panel of "so called" experts who seem to be from a local home or something, so inhuman and full of information from the last book they have read nothing more.

My husband and I married later in life than most, we were fairly quiet as individuals and we just met by a chance meeting nothing more. It was for both of us "love at first sight" and we had just so much in common it was magic. We hadn't been going out long when I said to him shall we get married and he said yes straight away so we did just that. Three friends only at a registry office and that was that, we moved in as a couple and here we are today, very happy indeed. I can't imagine a day without my husband and he without me.

Whilst we keep ourselves to ourselves, although we go to gardening clubs and craft clubs and the like we keep busy at home. Neither of us is very sexually active and it has never played an important part in our lives even when we were young. Your show on No Sex Relationships was very interesting and I thank you for actually producing and airing it, because I'm sure we are not alone in our way of lifestyle. It was so true in what you say about relationships and love and what others do has no bearing upon what you do. There are no ground rules other than your own and what is good for you. There is nothing in text books as to what you should or shouldn't do because it's none of anyone else's business.

It was so nice to hear your show Aunty Bronwyn it was both comforting and assuring even though we didn't need it, it never the less brought a warm understanding to what you said. Your show on "What Is Normal" proves exactly what is or isn't normal too, and you are so right in what you said even after reading the dictionary definition of it also as a comparison.

Thank you for your shows Aunty Bronwyn they are unique and genuine in their format and we both like listening to your family, it is so funny. God Bless Margery and Bill.

Women need a reason to have sex. Men just need a place.

Billy Crystal

100

I WAS LOSING MY SELF ESTEEM

Aunty Bronwyn we have a letter from Joel who writes. Aunty Bronwyn it is so true what you say about life, that at times we just end up in a place which is alien, cold and somewhere we didn't want to go, yet all of a sudden find ourselves there.

I had a series of setbacks in life it just seemed one thing after another, not catastrophic but enough to make you sigh to yourself quite regularly and start with as you keep saying often, "all that mind talk" – "the mind gremlins". Once you start muttering to yourself you are in reality affirming what has happened and where you are and then that slippery slope down life's helter-skelter starts to speed up. It happened to me, I got frightened to do things and say things and I started to dwell on "stuff", doesn't matter what it was I just dwelled on it. I even got to the stage where I selectively watched only certain programmes on television so that I didn't have to cope with any negative content that may have arisen.

If someone had told me how straight talking you were I doubt whether I would have listened to your programme in my state of mind, but they said it was funny so thinking I needed all the fun I can get I listened to it. It was funny, love your eldest sister and as for the twins, I had to smile. The way you deliver really hard information is just so correct, true and yet so compassionate that I felt energised for the first time for ages. I felt as though I'm not as bad as I make myself out to be. Your shows on Taking Charge", Loneliness, Self Esteem and the rest were just so concentrated it was the exact 'one shot' tonic I needed. Everything you said was doable, it was something I could implement without raising my own fear levels or getting nervous. I felt so livened after listening to your shows and that had real beneficial qualities all of its own.

It is so true what you say about self-esteem and what's around us, and who is around us. I just tried to make everything positive in my life, build up my own self-respect and allow events that were out of my control to go their own way. It took a little time to get this into an on-going habit, but I did and now I'm almost back on track and things are getting a lot better I have to admit. When you feel low even good things don't seem good so as you say again it is down to our perception.

Thank you, Aunty Bronwyn you've really turned my life around. Best wishes, Joel.

> *Always be your true self, and surround yourself with positive and supportive people.*
>
> *Amanda Lepore*

101

DOUBTING MYSELF

Aunty Bronwyn, a letter from Katheryn. Aunty Bronwyn there is so much truth in what you say about life and it is the little bits that seem to have the heaviest effect upon us. I come from a very negative family, nice people but eternal pessimists. When life goes well as you say we are all invincible, as soon as it doesn't go our way the true "us" comes to life and then it is virtually, "every-one for themselves", at least it was with me.

I was a follower, a procrastinator, a ditherer, an idler, and possibly loads more of those too. I used to get into such a complex tangle of options and permutations that at the end of the day I wasn't even quite sure who I was or what I really wanted to do. I think in hindsight I used to drive my friends mad discussing the most trivial things to the nth degree and then looking dazed and blank. I went to see a friend of mine and she was just about to listen to your show which was on self-doubt and procrastination and my friend looked at me with a big smile and a pointed finger and said, "does this ring a bell". It rang every bell to tell you the truth it was me in no uncertain terms.

You were right in that everyone who procrastinates or doubts hardly ever listens to themselves, they look outside of themselves as to what might happen elsewhere or permutations that no one can control thus they get so lost. It's not easy to just switch from one mode of years of expertly getting nowhere to saying yes or no and moving on in an instant, but it has made life better for me. I no longer get so tied up within myself, and I'm getting far more confident at making decisions based upon what's good for me.

Thank you Aunty Bronwyn I'm now a loyal fan of yours, your shows have made such a difference. All the best. Katheryn.

Procrastination is opportunity's assassin.

__Victor Kiam__

102

MARRIED AND WHITE. BLACK AFFAIR. CHILD ON THE WAY.

Aunty Bronwyn a moving letter from Val. Aunty Bronwyn I'm married with a lovely little girl. I decided to go back to work to get a better total income so that as a family we can enjoy a better standard of living. I then did the most stupid thing ever I had not only had a one night stand I did so unprotected and now I am expecting a child and the father is black. I perhaps could have gotten away with it otherwise, but the chances are the child will not be white.

It's a long and very pathetic story and I must take full responsibility for my actions and the hurt to my husband and daughter who will eventually find out. Guilt and remorse just don't come close to how I feel and what I wouldn't give to magic time back to before it happened. I was an ardent listener of yours and I really did think so seriously of contacting you directly with my dilemma as it had to be sorted sooner than later. You can't put a pregnancy on hold.

As if we don't have problems thrust upon us in life then I have to literally go and create one on a massive scale something that's going to be there for life. I eventually mustered up the nerve to tell my husband, that was the hardest thing I have ever done, I toyed with the storyline a million times and the permutations but eventually the truth was the best explanation. My husband was so shocked, he started trembling, he didn't lose his temper or shout or scream he just walked out the house and sat in the car. I was beside myself just what can I say more to appease the situation if at all? Nothing. Perhaps divorce was next on the cards, I was physically sick, I couldn't get my breath, where could I go who could I talk to, how do I explain to the world what I had done, I was going berserk I just couldn't think anymore, I was an instant wreck.

My husband came in eventually, went upstairs and moved into the back bedroom, I could hear him talking for ages on his phone. The next morning, he got up early went to work, not a word from him, came home played with our daughter not a word to me, went to bed, he had eaten before coming home so didn't eat his dinner. This went on for a few days then he said what do you want to do?

Aunty Bronwyn I had been mulling over what you had said in your shows when faced with problems like these and the bottom line of life is "love". However, it was trying in my mind to translate what I thought into what I wanted to say.

What you said was make a position in your "chance" platform to ask whoever it is to listen without interruption to your story, nothing more, just ask that of them. This could well be possibly the most important speech I've ever made or will make. He agreed.

I did as you had suggested I cut out all the hysterical waffle, all the sorry hype, all the I'm sorry for me, I'm sorry for you, I'm sorry for us, I've let everyone down, etc, no dramatics, no wild crying, I just told him exactly as it was and how it is and what I thought of him and our daughter and our life this far. Anything else as you mentioned hasn't yet happened so don't go overboard on "what I'd like for the future" (no stupid Hollywood stuff) – your own words Aunty Bronwyn because it doesn't exist, only the present exists, the past existed, that's it, it's no more.

So, speech started, floods of tears but no babbling crying, speech over. He sat completely motionless, I was trembling inside, my legs were weak, my palms were sweaty, I kept trying to get my breath, I was cold and shivering, all I could do was stare at my husband or was he to be my husband anymore, I was like the living dead. He then said, OK so where do we go from here now?

Did he mean divorce or as a couple, I didn't know how to answer, I was afraid to say anything. So, I said eventually what do you want, and he said I'm not sure, but we could still make a final go of it all, but you'll have to give me time I just really don't know how I feel at present I need to calm my mind down, just get to grips with it all.

We are still together, we did take the plunge and not make a secret of what had happened. The baby is due in three months it's a boy, both parents know, there you have it Aunty Bronwyn. I've aged mentally, our lives are relatively - almost back on track, the child will be loved, I still love my husband very much and think he is the most wonderful, brave and lovely man ever. As you say life is for tomorrow yesterday has now gone.

Your advice Aunty Bronwyn on how to break not so good news to the family was priceless. I got both parents and brothers and sisters together and said. I'm going to tell you something and it is not subject to comment or judgment nor phone calls afterwards. And I told them, again as you rightly said "don't pre-emt" anything just say it as it is, don't mention it's bad news or surprising news or this is going to be a shock or anything else, let them decide that themselves as that boosts your own resolve.

They were really very shocked, both parents speechless in fact. I know the story will eventually come out, but it's too raw for me to be the star turn for an audience I still need time and space myself at the moment.

Just a thank you Aunty Bronwyn for your advice in coping in difficult situations. I know it's different for everyone, but what you said was really spot on for that "once only speech" and I got it right, what more can I say. You are a wonder woman Aunty Bronwyn thank you so much I'm eternally grateful. Val.

***Having a baby is a life-changer.
It gives you a whole other perspective
on why you wake up every day.***

Taylor Hanson

103

JEALOUS BROTHER AND HIS WIFE

Aunty Bronwyn Anwar writes to us. Aunty Bronwyn I have two brothers and a sister, all married. With the exception of one of my brothers we all have children and we get on reasonably well with one another. The parents keep us all together although I'm not sure that will work when they eventually pass on.

Aunty Bronwyn I started listening to your shows when my wife had her last child. She used to listen to them then tell me all about them, so I eventually had to listen to them myself. I'm so pleased I did they have been a real eye opener in particular with regards the family type that I am from. You really have captured that very keenly. I am the youngest brother but my next brother up he and his wife have been trying for a child for years without any luck. Our parents don't help forever rambling on about it never giving them any peace. It turns out ironically that my brother can't father any children and my sister in law can't bear any children either so there's no option other than to adopt which neither want.

This situation has given rise to great jealousy in the family amongst them and the rest of us. They tell stories or make things up or are just off hand most of the time. To be honest I don't mind, but if you are going to be like that why even bother keeping in touch we have better friends than he and his wife. It was getting out of hand as many of these things do, my parents were forever whinging and that I can't stand either about how unfair and why and this and that and so it goes on.

AUNTY BRONWYN SPEAKING TO JOHN RUSHTON

It may seem quite petty but at the end of the day it was getting to me. Phone calls, texts, emails everything about the same revolving subject of which no one can help in any way, it is what it is. Your show on Taking Ownership and Love and Religion and Spirituality for me brought everything into light. My sister said to me don't upset the parents or they will cut you out of their will. And then I thought that's it, I've had enough. I sent an email to my brothers and sisters, I sent a letter to my parents literally telling them how disappointed I am with them and how heartless they are and left it at that. I also said I don't want a reply from any of my brothers or sisters because I don't care.

You know Aunty Bronwyn it made a world of difference. The family are a little closer than before and it shook my parents up, possibly too much but you know, me and my family are happy away from the pathetic small talk. Although what contact I do have is far better quality than before.

Thank you, Aunty Bronwyn you were right about families and how they think they can impose whereas they can't and shouldn't. It's wrong to be used because of something not so good. Best wishes Anwar.

104

CAUGHT MY BROTHER IN BED WITH MY GIRLFRIEND

Aunty Bronwyn a letter from Laurence. Aunty Bronwyn. I live at home with my brother there is a two-year age difference I'm 19 he's 21. Our parents are always away on cruises or holidays or something or other. As brothers we get on quite well but have never been that close for some reason. Two of my cousins have bothers they all get on really well with one another, we just don't. We don't argue but seem to live as lodgers and do what we have to do independently.

It's amazing how different people in the same family just can be, he's not very thoughtful and although we have a cleaner I still have to run around otherwise there would be clothes and towels everywhere. We both have girlfriends and keep to ourselves.

I came home unexpectedly and found him in bed with my girlfriend, they were both very shocked as I caused a scene and she dashed off very quickly. He said nothing other than it just happened. I was quite unnerved and just about lost all trust in him, I even had the lock changed on my bedroom door which phased him a little, especially as I told my parents when they phoned up and were not too pleased to hear that.

It was one of your shows Aunty Bronwyn on "Emotions" and "Self Esteem" that somewhat appeased the anger that I had within me that I just couldn't seem to dissipate. What you said on values, other people and perceptions made so much sense.

How other people either respect you or don't either because they don't like you or because they think they are better or just as sometimes happens are immune from other's feelings. Also, I'm best out of a relationship with my ex-girlfriend if she is such an easy target too, although it was never that serious never the less that's no excuse as to what happened.

It was a lesson and a half in growing up Aunty Bronwyn, and I did so appreciate your shows as they offered straight forward down to earth information that I would have never been privy to elsewhere. Just a big thank you to a now wiser teenager. Laurence.

Cheating is very rarely about the actual act of being with another person.

Emily V. Gordon

105

I'M HIV+ THE FIRST TIME I HAD SEX - ONCE

Aunty Bronwyn Wilhelm writes. Aunty Bronwyn I'm 17 and I'm HIV+. I think I've always known that I have been gay but supressed my feelings thinking that perhaps I'll find a girlfriend and then everything will be alright. I knew I was kidding myself as I think everyone does in life when you have certain feelings but don't want to admit why they are there. As I know to my detriment if you have strong feelings it is because you are either wired that way or you have them because it is you and trying to steer yourself away it is like asking a fish to climb a tree, it's not going to happen.

I was at a party and it was predominantly a gay party, I was with a good friend and staying at his house for the night. The night of the party I thought this is it I'm just going to let myself go and meet other gay people and was feeling quite plucky too, for me that is. The thought of sex and carrying condoms never entered into my mind. I don't drink so I was myself when I met a really nice guy who was gay, we just hit it off, he was gorgeous, the first kiss which was so memorable, the first time touching a guy and holding one I was all of a tremble, I thought yes this is it, I'm definitely gay and I love it I felt so emancipated and all of a sudden grown up.

We eventually went to a bedroom where we had full sex. It was amazing, one evening to change your life, little did I know how changed it would be. Eventually it was all over, and I had to leave with my friend. We exchanged numbers and my friend said I hope you used a condom, and I said I think he did, not knowing and just realising that fact.

AUNTY BRONWYN SPEAKING TO JOHN RUSHTON

It was all so much of a dream that it never entered my mind.

With exams coming up, sex, guys, life etc was all put on the back burner and I just revised until I had gotten through them. My friend said lets, go out and celebrate the finish of the exams which I agreed. We went to a gay bar and saw a drag act something that I'd never seen before and it was very funny, and I just liked the atmosphere. That evening he said he was going for a test at the local clinic as he was quite active on the scene and said why didn't I come along. I thought it a waste of time, but he said well in future if you go you know what to do, so I agreed and went with him. I was diagnosed with HIV+.

Your show Aunty Bronwyn on HIV+ was amazing as were some of the letters that people had written in about. Although I was shattered by the news, it's not the end of the world and one can lead a perfectly normal life and live to be a ripe old age. The moral is as you say always be prepared, I wasn't, I was a silly young guy who got overwhelmed and is now paying the price.

The emotional advice you gave Aunty Bronwyn was excellent, especially that of self-esteem and what other people need to know and other people being judgmental, etc. All that is very important because without self-esteem and not harbouring guilt or anguish life takes on a far better meaning.

I think many young guys could benefit from hearing your shows Aunty Bronwyn, as it would I hope stop what I had needlessly been through. Sex education isn't what it is cracked up to be despite the fact that it exists in various forms. Thanks Aunty Bronwyn, Wilhelm.

106

WIFE 33, THREE CHILDREN, DIES OF CANCER

Aunty Bronwyn Michael writes to us. Aunty Bronwyn you are so right when you say always live for the moment. I had a lovely wife, three fabulous children two boys and a girl and we were a happy family. My job wasn't the best in the world, but we coped and there was oodles of love all around. We never actually went short of anything although we couldn't afford great luxuries either. Having said all of that life was good, we had everything to live for and the children were bright and studious too.

During a routine check-up my wife was diagnosed with having breast cancer, it was not pleasant news but today if treated early on the success rates are very high. However, when she went to be further examined they found that the cancer had spread and that she needed a double mastectomy urgently, which happened. Then there was the ovarian cancer too that had developed, and then there was pancreatic cancer and so it went on. It was only a matter of time that my wife was engulfed with cancer and tragically died very shortly after her first operation.

Both our parents were excellent in every respect, even neighbours were marvellous, but that never equips you for looking after three children, working, giving them the quality time, they need and loving support and indeed the understanding of why mummy is no longer here. As for myself, I had to stay on top because I had three children who through no fault of their own needed total support to make a life for themselves at some future date, and that is what my wife lived for. That too takes its toll.

My wife used to listen to your shows Aunty Bronwyn and always found them very interesting, but I never listened myself. One evening shattered, I was downstairs, and I saw your information in a drawer, so I listened. It was so very helpful, the shows on Bereavement, Taking Ownership, Emotions, Whose Life Are You Living, God and Spirituality, they all had meaning and depth and filled quite a few gaps in my own thinking. It really did make a difference and I can understand why my wife now listened so much to your shows.

Thank you, Aunty Bronwyn for sharing this information, I'm sure many people will take to heart as to what you have to say on so many topics with your open mind and none judgemental approach. Your underlying theme is love throughout and that makes such a difference to the delivery of anything for without love you end up with the usual biased commercial mish-mash which is cheap and hollow like the daily national news on television, all totally biased and stilted.

Thank you for being different Aunty Bronwyn and your wise words they have made a difference already. God bless. Michael.

107

GETTING LOST IN LIFE

Aunty Bronwyn we have a letter here from Dawn. Aunty Bronwyn I'm single in my late thirties and I thought life had come to a full stop. I have been listening to your shows on and off for some time but like a lot of people one stores good ideas and information but unless you put it all to good use it just stays there, and nothing happens. I did one of the cardinal sins as you say and that is start comparing myself to others. I know we have to to some extent to qualify where we are in life but outside of that it then appears that others are far ahead or way behind and it leaves you exactly where you started – nowhere at all.

Once you have a negative aspect in your mind all the good points fade into oblivion and then you get a very staid mind set which leaves you feeling 'out of it' all the time. I was like this, it is really just so daunting having that feeling that there is nothing ahead of you or what their is doesn't hold water, it's all dull and uninspiring and everything else. The daily routine becomes a chore and you eventually lose whatever sparkle that you have, and you just can't seem to shake it off, it hangs around like dense fog.

I started listening to your broadcasts again and this time with definite intent and this time it really did make a difference because all what you had to say was about me, I was no longer just a listener I was "thee" listener and it was all very pertinent. You mentioned that the biggest problem you will ever have to face is yourself and that is so true, this whole state I was in was me intensified and I started it. It was me thinking internally and not externally, it was me narrowing life down to my small thinking whereas the permutations are infinitesimal and encouraging.

Your shows on Taking Ownership, Emotions, Loneliness, Mental Health all resonated so deeply as did the others that I thought it's time I really stopped moaning and started doing. Even just thinking like that makes a world of difference. Aunty Bronwyn, life has picked up considerably now because as I'm open to new things and events they present themselves to me. Before I couldn't see them for looking inwards and thinking "poor old me, what's to happen". I was the cause of my own dismay.

Thank you, Aunty Bronwyn you have really laid down the information for me to get life rolling again and it has. Thank you again. Dawn.

He who learns but does not think, is lost! He who thinks but does not learn is in great danger.

Confucius

108

IRRESPONSIBLE AND WEAK PARENTS

Aunty Bronwyn we have had a deluge of letters on this recent subject of parents and children on how ineffectual and thoughtless many modern parents seem to be. This is obviously an on-going topic and the gist of the letters have the following points raised.

That children are generally unruly.
Badly behaved in supermarkets and public transport.
Have no thought for others, seemingly self-consumed.
Parents allow their children to run wild with no thought about others around.
Generally, children don't listen to the parents and the parents rarely enforce what they say.
Few children are well mannered at all.
Many children appear as mini versions of neurotic parents.
Few children have any communication skills at all.
Many children are given a check list of how to live as opposed to allowing them to understand life.
Many parents are paranoid about life itself and this rubs off as nervous and diffident, unstable and unruly children.
Encouragement is quickly dashed by lists of 'be careful about' or 'don't do' to the extent that their undeveloped minds can't do anything positive.
School teaches children knowledge but little about today's life and expectations.
Political correctness is stifling development and growth, we are not a third world country, yet.
Mental health cases with children suffering from something or other is vastly increasing.
Many parents today are in themselves not so competent and treat children like mini adults which robs children of being a child and experiencing same.

109

BEING A FAILURE

Aunty Bronwyn, Johan writes to us. Aunty Bronwyn my family has a high degree of achievers in it, everyone has a really good job or has their own business or has some good credential as senior researcher at some well-known institute and so on. Then there's me, I did quite well at school went through University and came out with passes but nothing to showcase and still haven't got a clue as to what to do in my life.

I have left home and share a flat with two friends, it's not ideal but I do get peace and am away from the remarks of "your brother does this why don't you" or "ask your cousin for a job he has a big company" not a single word of encouragement. I know my parents care for me and they have even offered me money when I was a bit short, but I refused, I couldn't stand the possible backlash. At Christmas when everyone is together it is more of an ordeal than a happy family gathering.

One of my flatmates girlfriends was talking about your shows and how it had helped her through a trying time after her father had died and since then she listens all the time. I thought it could be just what I'm seeking too. It was, just a few minutes in to the show you identified what it was, all about situations that get people down. I listened to quite a few shows and still do now Taking Ownership, Failure itself, Self Esteem, Families, Relationships all resonated well within. Also, the Biggest Problem You'll ever face is yourself, and that is just so true.

As you say, "It's you arguing with yourself" and not getting a satisfactory answer that really gets to you.

You say so much Aunty Bronwyn but in reality, life isn't that complicated, it is our impression or perception of it and the fear of others around us that almost inhibits what we want to do for ourselves. The fear of comments and judgments that in reality is no one else's business yet we take it on board as if it is some subliminal authority and it is not in the slightest. Listening to your shows Aunty Bronwyn has literally changed how I think and that has made a world of difference I see things far clearer now and virtually take no negativity from others on board.

Thank you, Aunty Bronwyn, you have helped me no end in discovering myself and I'm far happier now than I have been for a long time. Kind wishes Johan.

> *A man can fail many times, but he isn't a failure until he begins to blame somebody else.*
>
> **John Burroughs**

110

COPING WITH DIFFICULT PEOPLE

Aunty Bronwyn we have a letter from Matthew. Aunty Bronwyn I'm not sure whether it was me or what, but I really have a hard time in dealing with objectionable people. I get so frustrated and deeply annoyed and I then I'd take it all to heart and then all day long I'm churned up inside, and sometimes it used to last for days. I'd even days after just keep churning it over and over again in my mind and get really annoyed all over again. I'm quite a placid person although I have no problems in making decisions in fact my job demands that.

For some reason it doesn't take much to wind me up, but from the moment it does I'm just out of it silently fighting back at whoever or whatever it was that had pressed my wrong buttons. A girlfriend of mine suggested that I listen to your shows as she was sure you had had one on Trapped Anger and Frustration, so I thought it could only do me good. I not only found that topic but quite a few associated with it and a few others that I was keen to listen to also.

You are so right in what you say. Don't ever give your authority away nor start to spar with others who will probably have a mono-minded thought process and will not be interested to listen to your point of view, even if they know it is right. Furthermore, you are not here to educate the world either, some people need to find out themselves – even the hard way. Don't also let your own ego and arrogance get a hold of you or that will be your immediate downfall. It's OK for others to be wrong they will find their own level eventually.

You are not here to put everyone right. Respecting yourself is paramount to being more secure in whom you are, and that has a great stabilising force within, no matter what situation you find yourself in.

Your views and thoughts Aunty Bronwyn have really helped me calm down and be far more rational and less insular than I used to be, and importantly not take things personally which is at times hard to do. I love your shows and some of your family really make me laugh. Thank you, Aunty Bronwyn. Matthew.

Problems are not the problem; coping is the problem.

Virginia Satir

111

SHYNESS AND TIMIDITY

Aunty Bronwyn I have a letter from Ethan who writes to us. Aunty Bronwyn I have all my life suffered from acute shyness and timidity. Imagine then someone saying to you we have put you down to do public speaking next week? That's what happened to me a while ago where I work in the creative section of our company. I have come up with the last four winning concepts and designs, so they asked me to tell everyone about it in the hope that my so-called genius will rub off. I died a thousand deaths within the next 15 seconds and I was running to the loo every 30 seconds. I can't tell you how extra creative I can really be at devising ways to have time off work to coincide with that date, but I couldn't go through with that, I will have to do it, another thousand deaths just struck again.

My friends and close work colleagues know what I'm like and even stand in for me at times where I have to give mini-presentations to clients, although after that I'm happy to talk clients from a sitting position delivering the concepts and the reasoning behind them. But they couldn't do this for me this time. Another thousand deaths just struck me. One of the girls I work with mentioned your shows and said try listening there may be something that could possibly help you other than hypnosis or ten boxes of Valium.

I did listen to your show on Shyness & Timidity and it did help me quite a lot to hear what you and others had had to say about events they had had to do. Your other shows on Taking Ownership really helped me too as did a number of others. As time was very short I really took to heart your advice and roped in two very close colleagues who had been with me throughout the projects and concepts and I was frank with them about the situation. They would introduce what I do and then at the end I would give a talk on me and what I do, which I could do. Again, I died a further one thousand deaths but this time the end result was just about doable, and I wasn't alone.

The day came, I was dying a thousand deaths every 15 seconds, I was having hot n' cold sweats and palpitations but was determined to go forward even if I collapsed and that was going through my mind continually. You did say Aunty Bronwyn go for it even if your voice is wavering and your legs are trembling, just do it. I did it, my turn came up and my colleague Simon said here's Ethan, just to tell you in his own words how he was inspired to design the recent winning designs. My voice was wobbling, and I had to hold the lectern to stop myself falling over but as I went on it really did get a little easier.

My boss congratulated me afterwards, he even said he was amazed that I had gotten this far and was delighted that I had tried so hard to make it all come together. I'm not sure that in any way I'm cured, but I do thank you Aunty Bronwyn for sharing your understanding and putting out those suggestions, they really worked for me and I have to be honest I feel quite proud of myself for having gone through with it.

 I'm just so thankful however that the following day was a Saturday as I was still all of a dither the following morning, even after a few drinks the night before.

Thank you, Aunty Bronwyn your shows are brilliant, and they have helped me overcome a number of things in my life. Best wishes. Ethan.

112

GAY MUSLIM - INBRED HATRED - A FAMILY DIVIDED

Aunty Bronwyn we have a letter from Amun who says. Aunty Bronwyn I'm a gay Muslim living in the UK, I have been here since I was little, and it is my home. I love it here I have a good job and great friends and have done well. My mother is French and my father Egyptian. All my other family are living just on the outskirts of Cairo and are a far cry away from living the quality and style of life I consider normal where I live.

On a recent visit to Cairo for a big family reunion I met the whole family, endless cousins and aunts and uncles it was awful, what dull boring narrow-minded people living in a microcosm of life shrouded in Islamic failure. Everyone telling me I'm going to die and how could I be like I am, and I just thought this is the whole problem. They are living a pathetic indoctrinated life struggling every day in a corrupt society, whilst I'm at the opposite end of the spectrum living in a civilised world and enjoying every minute of it, nice food nice clothes and they can't see any of it at all, they are all frightened and life is fear based. What God do they actually worship that delivers this?

I left early and told my parents it is the last time that I'm ever going back to Egypt and I don't want to see the family again, my family are the friends I have in the UK whom I have known for years and enjoy life with them around Muslims, Christians, Jews, I don't care. As for Islam you don't have to worship that religion to end up being substandard, what's wrong with everyone?

Aunty Bronwyn I was introduced to your shows by a friend of mine also from Egypt and she had been listening to them for some time as she had experienced something very similar. The Islamic abuse, you have to do this, you'll be punished all that evil dribble that they constantly eat sleep and drink. I listened to your shows especially Taking Control and God and Spirituality and Religions and Happiness and yes, it really put my mind at peace that I take control of my life not some outsourced garbage that doesn't support you but allows you to suffer. I feel so much better for listening to what you had to say, and you weren't judgemental either, it was all a matter of fact which I liked because the decisions were mine no one else's.

Thank you Aunty Bronwyn I wish you had an Arabic version of your shows because I'd send one to my family to listen to. I've told quite a number of my Egyptian friends to listen to your shows as a few of them suffer from abuse from their families. All the best. Amun.

113

DYSFUNCTIONAL CHILDHOOD LAID TO REST

Aunty Bronwyn we have a letter from Amelia. Aunty Bronwyn I'm now 36 and happily married with a son whom I adore and love. When I was small I lived in such an unstable world. My mother would just leave without warning and I had to stay with a neighbour, she wouldn't turn up to pick me up from school and after waiting for hours I had to go and stay with my gran and so it went on. I wasn't happy and always lived in fear that I'd be left alone one day and that would be it. There was nothing to look forward to and I lost faith in just about everything.

I eventually lived with my grandmother which was quite nice, she fussed around and tried to make up for what I had endured and really understood how I felt. I eventually got into university and possibly for the first time started to live my life even on a student's grant. That came and went, and I left and got a job where I met my husband. At the back of my mind I still couldn't stop thinking about my past, it was there to haunt me it was an indelible mark on my mind. Because of my past I was always there for my son, I would never ever let him down and I even looked out for other children in case their parents were late, it was something I had to do to appease what had happened in the past. A friend of mine who I had confided in regarding my past mentioned your shows and said why not listen when you have a moment you might get something from them. Eventually having put it off I did listen, and I wished I had listened a long time ago now. What you had to say about the past and where we live now was so true. We often know what to do deep down but just need that extra affirmation from someone who we trust or respect to make it happen, and Aunty Bronwyn you made it happen. The wisdom and knowledge you impart is so true and empowering, it's not just smart words but real heartfelt emotional words that had meaning.

You are right Aunty Bronwyn; the past is finished and has nothing to do with today. What you say is that today is the beginning of tomorrow as tomorrow is where we are going, yesterday we will never visit again. The future and my love are within me and living here and now, what was has all been laid to rest unless we drag it along with us. The past will do nothing and no matter what is done now it will never ever appease the past other than on an ego level, so it has to be let go of. If you respect yourself and life and those who are actively in it, then happiness will be allowed to blossom because that is where it is.

Happiness is the journey and not the destination. There's no happiness in looking at the past even if it happens to rekindle fond memories. Happiness and purpose only exist in the present where life is, so it needs to be nurtured every day no matter what.

Aunty Bronwyn a great cloud has been lifted from within, I can see everything so much more clearly now, regardless of the past the future is all mine and that is where I have the ability to empower my life and my love. Thank you Aunty Bronwyn I'm going to recommend you to all my friends. Kind regards Amelia.

114

WHINGING & POLITICAL CORRECTNESS TAKEN CARE OF

Aunty Bronwyn we have a letter from Bob. Aunty Bronwyn I was introduced to your shows by my girlfriend who was glued to listening to them. I can understand why as they are very informative and give a very direct approach to many aspects of life that have been hijacked by political correctness. I in fact love your no-nonsense comments and your anti political correctness stance.

The thing is I used to get so much politically correct conversations where I worked it used to drive me mad, I'd really get up tight and even come home fuming. I remember in your show about Political Correctness you said either ignore it or turn it back on to those who had made such a statement, but under no circumstances take it in as that is giving them your authority to upset you, they are not worth it. That made definite sense, so I thought I'd repost and not agree with what they said but in a genuine way, not just for the sake of it. I even used some of your statements Aunty Bronwyn like, "well that's your opinion but I don't value it at all", I've even said "I don't trust what you say", may be a bit strong but wow what a difference it made to these loud mouthed empty shells of nothingness.

Like many people they just put up with what others say but feel if they say something they will be taken to task, but now it's a case of I'll too say what I feel, appropriately and if they don't like it tough luck. It gets easier and what's more as you rightly said, you can always see the flaws of lack within politically correct people and what you also said is true too, they all seemingly have very bad relationships or none at all - I've noticed that. You are so right too in that small minded and useless people use Political Correctness as a card to try and get them what they want because they haven't the ability to do so through regular channels – they are failures.

Thank you, Aunty Bronwyn for just giving me the edge to stop allowing certain things to get to me. It may be small in the bigger picture of life but for me I was struggling with it. Thank you again from an ardent listener. Bob

115

UNEMPLOYED AND FEELING UNDERVALUED

Aunty Bronwyn we have a letter from Cheryl. Aunty Bronwyn I have had a job since leaving school and done well for myself. However out of the blue I was made redundant along with half the staff at the company I worked at. It was a bit of a shock, but the company wasn't doing too well for a number of reasons, we didn't know how badly until it was too late.

Being unemployed is no fun at all. Having to claim unemployment benefit is no joke. It is a game in itself and so intrusive and those who one has to see about helping to get you a job are just "check list chasers" nothing more themselves. Having to go and sign for money is demeaning especially as there is no intellectual capacity to talk on anything with anyone despite what they may say and the whole atmosphere is repressive.

I really dreaded my two weekly visits and the stigma of what I have to do and also the seemingly unfairness of those who can't even speak English hardly getting hosts of benefits, what's happening to everything. The whole thing is more than depressing, and everything that the Job Centre does is cheap beyond despair. If you have a brain that has two working brain cells then they can't help you at all, just go through stereotyped motions nothing more, all full of their own self-importance. A friend introduced me to your shows and I thought why not.

Aunty Bronwyn you should make your shows available to many who visit there because they would certainly induce some positivity in the midst of gloom and bureaucracy.

I loved your shows on Taking Charge and Being Unemployed, it was just nice to hear the realities of the facts as they are and what on one side people have to endure and the theory idiots who put it together on the other side. Typical Government run system would never stand up to a private system. Having said all of that Aunty Bronwyn, what you said really appeased the stigma I had and has gone a long way to just playing the stupid game whilst getting down to getting a job the best way I can. I feel so much better and feel more secure in myself. Aunty Bronwyn I'm sure you could teach the career counsellors or professionals some far better phraseology and improve the standard no end.

Thank you, Aunty Bronwyn I feel much better now and am sure I'll get a job very soon. All the best. Cheryl.

The search for justice and security, the struggle for equality of opportunity, the quest for tolerance and harmony, the pursuit of human dignity - these are moral imperatives which we must work towards and think about on a daily basis.

Aga Khan IV

116

CHANGING THE WAY YOU LOOK AT LIFE

Aunty Bronwyn we have a letter here from Charlie. I've have over the past three years had a bit of a roller coaster ride. I lost my job although fortunately got another one, not quite as good but I'm OK. I have been diagnosed with a long term medical condition although not too debilitating, both my parents have passed away and if that wasn't the last straw I've fallen for my best mate's friend, although not too phased by that in hindsight.

If I start in reverse order I hadn't had a girlfriend for quite some time now, I just didn't have the interest, my last relationship just fizzed out and that was it. My best mate's friend is gay they have been mates since school so know just about everything about each other. It didn't really occur to me anything other than he was what he was until at a party one evening I was alone and he came up and spoke to me which I was thankful for, better than being the proverbial wallflower.

The party was full of straight people although he knew most of them and was quite popular with just about everyone. We just really hit it off so well and as the evening went on I was getting somewhat more and more attracted to him. Long story short he went off eventually to socialise but said let's meet for a drink, we did, had my first guy to guy kiss, I felt like a teenager again starting out all over. As much as I liked it all it still took a little time for it to all sink in.

We are a little more than friend's now and my best mate thinks it's really funny but in a nice way, he can't get over it.

AGONY LETTERS

We keep saying it will be him next.

I was diagnosed with a long-term condition that provided I keep active and look after myself nothing too drastic should happen, so I have to be thankful for that, but it took a bit to sink in. Both my elderly parents died within six months of each other and whilst they were elderly they are your parents and now there is that void, but I got over it and the little inheritance didn't go amiss. I lost my job suddenly, the company was taken over, it was relocated, and I really didn't want to move so redundancy happened. I did get another job not quite as good but nearer to home and so it has its good points.

My new boyfriend seems strange saying that, told me of your shows so I listened with him and I really liked them, they were very informative and down to earth. Taking Ownership, Life from A Different Perspective, Bereavement and the others all made a substantial difference to how I thought and felt and really got me out of the typical stereotype thoughts that many seem to have.

Thank you, Aunty Bronwyn for your shows and the humour, I love the twins it makes me smile. What you had to say really encapsulated my life over the last few years and has put it into a degree of perspective, not being so fragmented as it was. It has made me look at life from not only a different perspective but from a different me because I have changed and like a computer you do need to update the software, or it just doesn't work properly. It's taken some time Aunty Bronwyn and a few big issues in my life to make all this happen, but it has been worth waiting for and just being grateful each day makes a world of difference. Thank you for that from the newest gay on the block. Charlie.

FOUR SISTERS – THREE SLIM AND FAT ME

Aunty Bronwyn Judy writes to us. Aunty Bronwyn I've been pondering for some time about writing to you, but in the end, I just had to tell you my story as it may help others. I am one of four sisters, we really get on well together, there's a year apart between each one of us. However, and here's the bugbear, they are all so slim and curvy whilst I'm the endlessly podgy one who is not so curvy but rotund. Whereas they can dance and do gymnastics and climb up trees there I am at the back red faced gasping and panting and sweating about to collapse or make something collapse because of my weight. My sisters can get into each-other's clothes, I couldn't even get into pillow case.

My other sisters were sympathetic and went out of their way to help me or even not do things because they knew I couldn't or not without a great deal of stress and strain so they all thought otherwise. Academically we were all about the same and did well. My other sisters had boyfriends before I did, and, yes, I was the proverbial clumsy girlfriend that went red and silly and embarrassed and anything else that you could conjure up or become. It wasn't bad, it wasn't that I was left out, it was that I was just the way I am and that's not compatible with what others do including my sisters. Away from them I was fine, but I still liked being with them because it was fun.

A friend of mine told me of your shows and that she was a regular listener of them, she had said that she had learned a lot and it had helped her even though she said she didn't think she needed any help. I listened, and I have to say the same.

AGONY LETTERS

I needed to learn to love myself for whom I am and not just accept that I am what I am but deep down not quite like it for which as you rightly mention there is a big difference. You go straight for the jugular Aunty Bronwyn, but it is so true, and you never say anything hurtful. I did really need to be able to say no, and I did really need to be able to say you do that I can't without feeling embarrassed or letting myself down. Every situation is what it is and therefore no excuses other than the truth need be applied as a smokescreen. I had been utilising so many smokescreens and untruths just to appease myself it wasn't true.

The vast majority of people will accept you for who you are, if you do, if you don't, then the chances are they won't anyway because they will subliminally pick up what you are hiding or running away from. But Aunty Bronwyn that's all stopped thanks to you, I am now the 100% version of myself no cover up nothing, it's all me and what a difference. Even my sisters said I had a sparkle that I hadn't had before. I actually no pun intended feel lighter in myself, instead of dragging my body around I am my body and it is fine just the way it is, as my boyfriend will tell you. It's amazing what this knowledge can do it increases your self-esteem and presence and stops all that hiding behind others or people or whatever it is, no reason to anymore.

As you say Aunty Bronwyn, where the mind goes the body follows and that's just so true. A heavy dull mind with negative thoughts creates a vehicle which is mirror image of it, which it is not so.

Thank you, Aunty Bronwyn I'm not only happy with whom I am but life all around me as I now can reflect what I don't want and be who I do want and what's more I will no longer farm out my thoughts as to what others think and say, I am me and that's enough. Thanks again Aunty Bronwyn big hugs Judy.

118

JEWISH AND GAY – THE GOOD AND NOT SO GOOD

Aunty Bronwyn we have a letter here from Samuel. Aunty Bronwyn I had been living a lie now for some time and it was getting to me. I come from a quite conservative Jewish family which was tolerable up until now. I had had gay feelings for quite a while and recently at a family reunion I met a cousin of mine who is gay and has come out to his family. I mentioned to him my feelings having questioned him endlessly about his feelings etc, and I decided that I was probably gay. We arranged to meet up and he took me to a gay club, I was so nervous, but I loved it, I liked his friends and his parents are amazing, everyone was laughing and having a good time, something that I had not enjoyed for ages. My mind was all of a swirl. My cousin's parents are really cool about the whole thing and even about me which was quite exhilarating in a way being accepted for who I am just like that.

However, the flip side of the coin was not so exhilarating at all. I made a stance and told my parents who went absolutely mental. My cousin had said that before telling his parents he had listened to a number of your shows Aunty Bronwyn which included Taking Ownership, Love, Being Gay, etc and it helped him no end. The fact he said that he at the end of the day didn't have to use any of the information he had gleaned was immaterial because it has given him peace of mind and made him more secure and happy about who he is.

I duly listened to the shows and I can really say they were brilliant as I had never thought that way nor had what you said even cross my mind although in effect is was all common sense. Armed with this new information I told my parents out right in front of my two brothers at the table. What an explosion, my two brothers dashed to their bedrooms straight away leaving my parents to fight off the invading Star Wars Battleship Galactic single handed and a good job they were doing too.

It was momentous I couldn't get a word in to say all the things that I had stored up, and from a "supposedly" loving son reduced to something the devil had spawned in an instant. To cut a long story short I ran out, phoned my cousin who lives not too far away and stayed that night at his house. The next day I returned and fortunately no one was at home, so I took some clothes and stayed another two nights at my cousins. I never answered my mobile from my parents calls. I eventually returned to somewhat distraught parents but still ready for showdown part 2. I said I was leaving for good and not returning and going to tell the whole community how evil they were I really went to town, which changed their minds somewhat, at least temporarily. I'm still at home I rarely speak to my parents or my brothers. I said some very horrible things which I will apologise for but not just now as it really shocked them to the extent they have I think reviewed who they are.

I want to move out but can't just yet. If I can get a flat share I'm making the move as soon as possible. My parents won't accept me, I'm there under sufferance so I don't need people like that even parents as all they do is bring me down. Like my cousin I really feel so much better for having heard your shows Aunty Bronwyn, everyone needs to be who they are everyone needs the best chance you can get and as you say where is the love. I really feel so hurt and unloved where their pride is more important than me. It's my life that I have to live it's not that

I've harmed them or stolen from them, being gay isn't a choice you are what you are you don't decide to make the choice? I grown-up by about 10 years in the space of a week and feel like it.

Life isn't ideal by any means at the moment, but one thing is for sure I know where I'm going even though I now have to do it all alone. I feel confident in myself and I feel comfortable in my own skin. I just don't feel comfortable at home which feels alien and that I'm an intruder. Thank you, Aunty Bronwyn your shows really pin pointed the bottom line which has been negatively crossed. I'm worth more than how I'm treated, and no one should be put down because of the failings of others. That will change. Thanks again Aunty Bronwyn. Big hugs Samuel.

It's simple, if it jiggles, it's fat.

Arnold Schwarzenegger

119

IT'S MY LIFE NOT YOURS

Aunty Bronwyn Anabelle writes to us. Aunty Bronwyn I come from a very privileged background, the family are wealthy, and I've had just about everything that I want. My brother has sports cars that his friends are envious about and who will probably never be able to own their own ever. I've never had expensive taste like that although I've had the best in whatever I wanted. I did well at university, my brother just flunked around but then he'll never work and doesn't have to. I suppose that I don't have to work either, but I choose to I just need to do it for me.

About a year ago I met a guy at my company, Jason a senior designer who I quite fancied yet despite requests to go for a drink after work he refused with some excuse or other. One of my colleagues who I confided in said he was frightened of me because I was so out of his class, so I took the bull by the horns approached him and said we are going out tonight for a drink, no excuses. On hindsight it was sad and amusing he was so nervous and really in an uncomfortable position. After a couple of drinks, and he rarely drinks, he opened up that he has to take care of his mother as she has a medical condition and he had had to make last minute arrangements with his sister who lives quite away to stand in for him.

I'd never had to experience what he had had to give up as whatever I needed we got someone to do it and that was that. He was just so lovely and kind and thoughtful not like anyone I had met before. We met a few more times and he became much more comfortable. I insisted I pay for the drinks and dinner because I knew he had obligations linked to his finances and wouldn't take no for an answer despite his protestations. Eventually I insisted that I see his mother at home. He was even more nervous than ever but said OK. His mother was so sweet and lovely, such a nice lady and she said she was so pleased that he had got a nice girlfriend and that he spent too much time with her and not going out, which caused him a great deal of embarrassment.

It was my turn now to invite him to see my parents. It was a nightmare, they couldn't stand him, my brother was rude, and it was an endurance test to the end. I could see Jason was uncomfortable, but he seemingly took no notice whatsoever and just carried on as if what they said was of no importance, it wasn't. He really surprised me when it was time to leave when my parents said condescendingly I hope you enjoyed the evening knowing he hadn't and he said no, not at all, and just stood looking at them. For the first time ever, they really didn't have an answer to give. After a few seconds I said right we must go and that was it. Far from being upset I really felt elated and so proud of him that he had this real depth that I had never seen before. He wasn't being rude just blatantly honest, and my parents knew it.

On the way back, I asked him if the evening was that bad and he said it was. The food was lovely, the surroundings sumptuous but her parents weren't that nice. They made no effort and seemed to amuse themselves by the whole occasion, and I realised he was so right.

When we got back to his house his mother was up and he said he had had a great evening, although she said quietly to me she doubted it by the look on his face which made me smile. I told her what he said, and my parent's reaction and she started laughing quite a lot. Now you know Jason she said. She said since he had been listening to Aunty Bronwyn with her they had both changed their thoughts and feelings about many aspects of life, and then she said you should listen to her too.

At home my parents weren't at all happy, but I had to laugh, it's not often that I had seen them lost to know what to do. They had been rejected. They then started saying he's not the right sort, he's not this or that, so I put all that to a close and said he's everything you aren't except the money and I really like it and went to bed.

The next day I had the third degree, this rejection by a 'commoner' had really gotten to them, so I just walked out and went to see Jason as it was Saturday. I said to him your mother had mentioned about Aunty Bronwyn and he said we should listen tonight if you like. I now know why Jason despite his faults speaks his mind, and just why he can say what he does without fear of any reposting or anything else.

It was so uplifting for me too. I even view life differently now myself. My parent's constant negativity I put into place straight away when I got home and said "this is my life not yours" let's keep it that way.

So far, we are getting closer and closer to each other. Aunty Bronwyn you have really helped close that gap between our respective backgrounds. I know it shouldn't make any difference, but it did and now it is as none of it matters. I feel so much better and I really don't care if we eventually have a cheap registry office marriage with a couple of friends Jason has brought such a new meaning to my life, something that had always been missing. Thank you, Aunty Bronwyn for your words of wisdom, Big hug Anabelle.

120

LISTENING AND TALKING

Aunty Bronwyn we have a letter from Byron. Aunty Bronwyn I'm one of those people who for whatever reason gets seemingly ignored or talked over or not listened to. It's not the end of the world but at the same time it makes you hold back or become slightly reticent at saying anything profound, leaving talking to just odd comments. I'm not rejected or spurned at all in fact I'm just about always included in whatever is going on. I couldn't put my finger on what it was, but it was a real situation never the less.

After listening to one of your shows on "listening" what I found was that when talking in a group I would give a factual response whereas others gave an emotional response based upon their perspective. I wouldn't do that, I'd say it as it was, and that for some reason it would have precluded others saying what they thought and relegated it to a nothingness i.e. they just wanted to speak so curtailed my conversations. I had been listening to your shows for some time Aunty Bronwyn and the ones on communication and respect confirmed what I thought. Listening is an almost dying art form everyone wants to comment, say their piece, get their voice aired but few actually listen to what is being said. I think it goes further that people when reading read into whatever the subject matter it is what they want and not what is required.

The absence of me not saying anything isn't a problem, if others want to chat on via their own thoughts that's fine. What is interesting when they have exhausted their dizzy banter they then ask me my comments as if they are seeking an affirmation of what they have said or an aspect of clarity that they may have missed. I'm no guru that's for sure but what I say is far more wholesome than their generally woolly conversations.

Your show on Taking Ownership and about 'turning what you don't like around on to itself' is just so enabling in that if you allow or accept something to perpetuate then it becomes the accepted norm then you only have yourself to blame. As you rightly say you can't carry on blaming everyone else for things if you make no effort to effect change yourself. You are so right too Aunty Bronwyn, that if a group of people no matter how nice they are continually rub you up the wrong way, what are you doing with them when there are millions of people out there who will be more or less as you want.

Taking ownership as you say is really what life is all about, and I can see that I was just being a passenger in my own journey not making any headway regardless of what it was.

It wasn't that others didn't like me it was that they needed interaction to give themselves some kudos in the process. Whilst I was happy to be as I was in their company I couldn't have it both ways, not to speak, then just decide to speak when I felt in the mood.

It is a delicate balance between joining in and occasionally joining in, either way is OK, but others need to know which is it as they are not sure as to how to interact with you, and at times become a little desperate themselves in the conversation stakes.

All your shows Aunty Bronwyn have some good advice or structures and the letters you receive are all helpful and informative of how others have had to steer or engineer their lives in a better way. Thank you, Aunty Bronwyn for your shows they are really great. Best Byron.

121

LIFE'S ANGST

Aunty Bronwyn this is one a number of letters on the very same subject Angst, this one is from Rebecca. Aunty Bronwyn from a very early age all I have seemed to know is Angst, there has always been some sort of worry, some sort of in trepidation, some sort or unease whatever it was there was always something that took the edge of life. Yes, I did have good moments but by and large they were all short lived. You are so right when you say your family can be responsible for how you start-off in life and how you develop, and I think some are so browbeaten that in their teens they never get out of it. The education system today is so constipated and run by politically correct idiots that dwell of theory that it is a far cry from producing healthy children with a balanced outlook on life and I agree with you on the negativity of political correctness it is evil in every form.

I was a product of all the above, my parents weren't bad but they in all honesty didn't do much for me anyway, I don't like saying that but in hindsight it was a bit of a bumpy childhood and my teens weren't much better. I eventually left home which was traumatic as coming from a negative existence one never thought things would be better, but after having moved I just wish I had done it years earlier. You are so right Aunty Bronwyn that many people live in a cocoon and don't realise that there is a life outside of it.

After a choppy succession of relationships, I eventually found a lovely man who saw through the façade of negativity and was quite blunt when I started to ramble on about certain things by stopping me dead and saying I'm not here to listen to your past excuses I'm here to listen to you now. This was a revelation in that I had to think of creative things and not dwell on the past. A friend introduced me to your shows Aunty Bronwyn, it was weird, my boyfriend, now my husband, on one hand challenging me and on the other your shows just literally outlining all the negative things I had been doing.

Far from being a difficult challenge it was all very much an emancipation of myself, it brought home how I had been conditioned albeit circumstantial to think in a certain what, a way that was dull and dowdy and negative and had no future within it. Your shows on Taking Ownership, Relationships, The Family, Failure, in fact all of them were just so brilliant in that in an instant it really did change my thought patterns. My boyfriend noticed a change and that I was laughing more and not taking notice of all the small negative stuff which before I would dwell upon and make into some blockbuster movie.

I can't tell you Aunty Bronwyn what a transformation it has been, and I can't even now imagine what I was like. You are so right it takes just a few little moves to change everything a great deal. As you say it takes that small pin to burst a big balloon nothing more, nothing psycho-complex, just do it, and bang it's gone in an instant. I'm expecting twins now and I'm promising them myself the best I can possibly do, no overbearing parenting as they need to develop themselves into who they may be, but just give them the support and love in order to do it.

Above all let them grow up in an environment of hope and positivity, even though at times we all go through "stuff" just keep on the high side of life as you mention Aunty Bronwyn because on the high side you can see for miles, on the low side all you see is the undergrowth.

Thank you, Aunty Bronwyn (and my husband) for giving me that one chance to make a break and I'm just so thankful when the opportunity knocked I opened the door. God bless you.

***Too often we underestimate the power
of a touch, a smile, a kind word,
a listening ear, an honest compliment,
or the smallest act of caring,
all of which have the potential
to turn a life around.***

Leo Buscaglia

122

THE TALE OF HAVING ENDLESS BOYFRIENDS

Aunty Bronwyn Angelina writes. Aunty Bronwyn what can I say I've made such a mess of my life so far. I've gone around since my late teens searching for a good boyfriend and I have found not one but quite a few all of whom I have dismissed as not being suitable. My girlfriends have almost lost patience with me as I meet someone then I see someone else and them someone else and progressively I've dumped one in favour of another. It came to a head a while ago when two of my boyfriend's met by chance, and there was an altercation where I came of the worst.

My father was at a friend's house and in general conversation sons and daughters came up, my father saying that I was driving him mad because no one is ever suitable, and I was going through boyfriends like a sale frenzy. One of the gathering said had he ever listened to Aunty Bronwyn, he hadn't but thought he'd have a listen. One of the programmes was on Relationships and he told me to listen to it as he thought I needed to know. I did listen to it and I actually felt quite embarrassed as it described me perfectly.

The bottom line about people like me is they are selfish, self-centred, thoughtless and are the main reason why we fail ourselves. All of the failures that I had experienced there was one common denominator and that was me, it was not any of the boyfriends at all, even if they weren't the right ones, it was me. It was me forever searching for better and better and seeking material aspects rather than the love and kindness and humanity which they possessed.

AUNTY BRONWYN SPEAKING TO JOHN RUSHTON

I listened to your other shows Aunty Bronwyn and they certainly put the perspective of my life back on track and how much of a low life person I had been playing people off with other people then moving on. It had actually become a habit and like a habit or a drug fix you just can't stop and then you lose all credentials of both yourself, and what you set out to do because your focus leaves you too. It is the "carrot and the donkey" scenario nothing more it never ever stops.

I grounded myself for a while just having nights out with my girlfriends and one night I met a really nice guy who took me off guard, he was lovely, and I started to feel very nervous that I might revert back to how I was and was this guy only nice now and would I meet someone potentially better. I was almost at a panic stage with myself. Anyway, armed with you Aunty Bronwyn in the back of my mind almost telling me off – in a nice way – I persevered and now it has been over six months we have been going out and I don't want to look at another guy at all.

It has made such a difference Aunty Bronwyn, listening to what you had to say and it was so simple and doable too.

I wish you were available for everyone because there's nowhere where you can get that information presented as it is just straight to the point and no marketing or media waffle or effected people telling you all sorts of rubbish. I love your eldest sister also Aunty Bronwyn, I feel I might have ended up like her had I not heeded your advice and I love the twins it really makes me laugh. Thank you, Aunty Bronwyn Angelina.

123

LIFE HYSTERIA

Aunty Bronwyn Joanna writes to us. Aunty Bronwyn it's amazing how if you are not careful you can get sucked into an area of life that has nothing to do with you and yet you make it your own concern thus adding additional stress and burdens to you own already busy life.

You are so right that we make our friends and family (those who care about us not necessarily blood related) that tend to fall within our own thinking and understanding and lifestyle. Whilst this is good it can also have its drawbacks in that everyone can start discussing matters that are inconsequential, unimportant and have no bearing whatsoever on our lives, in fact it goes to show what hollow and shallow lives at times we lead. I had been listening to your show on Taking Ownership and a few others, and all of a sudden it really hit home that much of my own mental health and sleeplessness was of my own doing.

I was going through a difficult time for a number of reasons and everything seemed to be stacking up and of course at night it just came to a point where my mind wouldn't stop talking in my head, some nights worse than others. Taking Control as you rightly mentioned means stop reading stupid stuff about stupid people doing stupid things which if they died would have no effect upon you whatsoever, nor are you benefiting from them anything they do.

Furthermore, the press and media coverage of anything is so grossly manipulated that there is a very fine line between fact and fiction, superfluous stuff having been added to it to make a story that bears no or little resemblance to the actuality of it all.

AUNTY BRONWYN SPEAKING TO JOHN RUSHTON

I made a concerted effort to stop reading all the celebrity magazines, stop watching all the similar shows or interviews, stopped looking at the news on a regular basis as it rarely changed often it being regurgitated to the extent it was facile. Changed the programmes I watched to a more wholesome variety and of interest to me. Stopped my calls to friends who talked on nothing but gossip apart from a brief "hi how are you" at times, changed or disengaged from any conversation that implicated anything about negativity and you know what Aunty Bronwyn, I'm a million times better now than I was. My problems haven't vanished, but I can see and feel better in my mind's eye as to what I have to do, and I just do it.

You are so right in that what we feed our mind, so we become and are ourselves. We become vessels of nothingness and topped up full of the most useless pathetic information that serves absolutely no purpose whatsoever. If we put the interest of people, we don't know ahead of our own lives it doesn't say much about us or how we think and feel. Nor does it bode well with those around us listening to them talking about other people or situations as if it is pivotal to life, whereas in reality it has no value whatsoever, and many of such people are unstable and of low value themselves.

Aunty Bronwyn I had to write and just mention this because it really has made a difference. I had gotten into a habit of following useless people for my own entertainment, but it served no purpose and now I feel so elevated that I really don't care about any of them anymore and I can focus on those that do mean something in my life. Thank you, Aunty Bronwyn. Joanna.

124

AM I BI-SEXUAL OR AM I PLAYING THE FIELD?

Aunty Bronwyn Nathan writes to us. Aunty Bronwyn for years now I have been living with the thought that I am a bi-sexual man in that I go with men and women in phases. The emotional experience is different in both cases and to some extent that is what was triggering off periods of time with each type of partner, I was becoming an expert of suddenly switching my stance and I was actually getting a little bit smug with myself that I knew what floated each partner type's boat.

The upshot of all this is that it after time has subliminally backfired as gay or straight people know what they are respectively looking for, and as for myself I was locked into a nothingness that provided only a temporary respite, the highs being high but the lows being low. Nothing was satisfactory, and it was always choices and circumstances and availability but nothing that was emotionally satisfying, it was a predominantly a lust-based scenario.

Just in conversation a friend had mentioned your shows and I thought they sounded interesting, so I thought I'd give it a listen and I was quite surprised at what I heard, what you said made perfect sense in every case. The shows on Taking Ownership, Sexuality, Loneliness all resonated well within. In fact, my dilemma the one that I had been struggling with pertaining to my sexuality or experiences had been answered. I had to make a choice based upon what I knew was me even though there was perhaps always going to be that side that looked the other way. In the past I had just followed what came easiest but that never ever lead to a satisfactory relationship. Now I had to literally work on it all and make it my sole responsibility and build up a relationship.

It wasn't easy, but your words sounded in my mind Aunty Bronwyn and that helped too, it helped to affirm who I was and what I stood for not some "easy come easy go" person but someone with stability and purpose. I now have a very stable relationship and the desires to flip the coin very seldom raises its head, and is quite controllable, more out of habitual giving in than anything else.

Thank you, Aunty Bronwyn I just needed to hear what you had to say to put into place what I needed to do, and you certainly said it all. Thank you again. Nathan.

You cannot escape the responsibility of tomorrow by evading it today.

Abraham Lincoln

125

BREAKING UP THE RELATIONSHIP

Aunty Bronwyn Eric writes to us. Aunty Bronwyn I have been with my partner now for about 8 years and like all relationships they start off in a flurry then it needs work, time and effort to allow it to develop into something sustainable, loving and above all into a strong friendship. As you rightly say Aunty Bronwyn, any relationship that is devoid of the friendship element just loses its power and energy and eventually you end up as two people cohabiting, which is what has happened.

Your show on Relationships succinctly outlines the many permutations of people originally "shacking up" just because they can, where the relationship is young and although relatively sincere it hasn't had time to blossom and unfortunately because of the parameters never does so. I've seen this with a number of friends around me and thought it would never happen to me, but it has. You are so bang on that many "nice" people make that mistake that life together would be good, but in reality, it is more of a convenience against loneliness, sharing food, convenient sex, being with someone to go to the cinema with, holiday with, wherever. Although this is the ideal for all relationships, if that 'spark' or real 'love' isn't there then it just fizzles out as you develop more and more self-interests and the together interests just get less and less, and what is there is just the convenience factor.

I was spending more time with my mates or working late as coming home wasn't the high agenda it used to be.

AUNTY BRONWYN SPEAKING TO JOHN RUSHTON

My partner was doing the very same thing and your show really brought all this home. Aunty Bronwyn what you do in all your shows is just "highlight" without bias or judgment areas that we need to listen to. We don't need endless "self-help" books or anything else as I think many people know what to do they just want a nudge or affirmation and that's it off they go and with a better heart too, than contemplating endless pages of mumbo jumbo. Just listening to your shows on the respective topics and a few mins in and there you are it's all there for you.

It does take a bit of courage to broach the subject of possibly separating, but you even covered that in another show to make it as amicable as possible where both parties deep down know it is the right thing but still don't like admitting to it. It can be still traumatic but starting on the right foot – if there is one – and not apportioning blame or trying to make the other partner low and still offering support really does help a lot. It is as you say Aunty Bronwyn essential to keep that support there and keep your spirits high and don't let emotions take over.

I was appreciative of your comments for the following, you are saying. Even if one partner does take it exceptionally badly and goes off the deep end and drama acts, still keep that offer of help and support open, even after they may have said they don't want to speak to you again in the extreme case. There are no exceptions in life where keeping a positive mind will not help you. If by chance you feel that you should be more upset than you are, don't berate yourself or try to induce or feign distress or tears just accept you are the way you are and move on.

Aunty Bronwyn, these snippets of information are invaluable because when you are going through "stuff" you just don't think of them. But being for-armed makes a world of difference and you can be more cool and calm and not say things out of turn or that you may regret.

As you say separating is an essential element of moving forward, albeit unpleasant, it is better to separate than stay together unhappily, because that is a life of self-repression, and undue duress. Being single many not be ideal either but as you mention our lives are under our control as is predominantly that of Loneliness too.

Thank you for your shows Aunty Bronwyn, and your unbiased information, allowing the listener to do with as they feel. Very best wishes Eric.

> *Your pain is the breaking of the shell that encloses your understanding.*
>
> *Khalil Gibran*

126

WHEN LIFE LONG FRIENDS FADE AWAY

Aunty Bronwyn June writes to us. Aunty Bronwyn I am so thankful that I had caught your show on Friendship and Friends as there had been an issue on my mind for some time and I just couldn't get over it.

I have two friends whom we all have kept in touch with each other since we were at school. One lives reasonably close by and we meet for coffee and a good natter relatively frequently. The other lives now quite a way away although we did speak often by phone. We all have busy lives and we have families of our own, our respective children are all in a similar age group, so we know by and large what they could be going through at school and adolescence etc. Over the past two years I have if I am to be honest lost both friends in as much as we never meet up nor do we speak. Even after a quick phone call and a brief but nice chat nothing, no reciprocation nothing.

It's amazing that we have all been so close for over twenty-five years, and then it all went cold. I know things happen and life evolves and that nothing ever stays the same yet I always though friendship was a little thicker than that. I was wrong. Your words however Aunty Bronwyn firstly brought what I had enjoyed for over 25 years into perspective, a really good hearty friendship. That must be treasured at all costs and it needs to be kept within the context of all of us and never to let that image and those memories get tarnished by what has happened today.

AGONY LETTERS

The other point you raised was that everything in life has a life expectancy. We meet people for days – as on holiday – weeks, months, years, possibly life, but as life is organic and evolves so do we as people. We can outgrow those around us because our life status changes, and thus what we do and how we think is either elevated or even lowered so it places our expectations on a different level. Similarly, others have exactly the same situation too, where their lives for one reason or another are changed by circumstances – good or bad- and thus they now view life differently and all what's in it. The theory is possibly we are friends so whether it's good or bad news we should remain friends, unfortunately that is not the case in the vast majority of situations.

I still feel slightly slighted by the sudden dropping off of the friendship that existed and possibly my own expectations as you say have been hurt not deliberately but what I would have liked in my "fairy tale" thoughts to have lasted. I do relish your thoughts and explanations Aunty Bronwyn, as it has really helped me come to terms with what has happened and not allowed it to fester within. I'm not even tempted to phone anymore although I may at some stage do so even if to just say "hi" and not expect any further chat.

What you say about expectation Aunty Bronwyn is so so true, that if we are not careful we can shoot ourselves in the foot by expecting more that we should then feel let down, whereas things are as they are and that's it. Excess thinking only goes on to raise other issues and raise other problems and that then solves nothing, but by default brings unrest where it shouldn't exist.

Thank you, Aunty Bronwyn for your take on friendship it has made a world of difference. Best wishes. June.

127

TOXIC FRIENDSHIPS

Aunty Bronwyn we have a letter from Clarissa. Aunty Bronwyn I was listening to your shows and came to the conclusion that many problems we face all emanate from a similar source and require the same solution. How we look at life or how we fare is basically the same regardless of what we are going through.

For quite a time I was living in a part of life that had little meaning. I just didn't seem to get the enjoyment or happiness out that I thought I should. I know what you say about happiness and I totally agree that happiness is a choice only we ourselves can make, but I wasn't actually unhappy, just feeling that I was losing out on something, but couldn't put my finger on it. Although I'm not in a relationship at the moment, your show on Relationships coupled with the one on Taking Ownership hit home. It was where I had allowed myself to be that was the problem. I was surrounded by very negative people, predominantly single and around my own age, let's say a few years over 33. It wasn't that they are bad people, but looking coldly they were all harbouring past failures, the thought that they were single in themselves, they were somewhat staid in what they did, and your show on Loneliness outlined that trait of meanness that was evident in all of them, not in a nasty way but all were calculating.

I had to re-check myself a few times to make sure that I wasn't making all this up, or trying to fit pieces together, but it seemed to be the correct assumption. So, what do I do now? At first, I thought I'll try and change my lifestyle possibly to a one that has more spontaneity in it and less of a planned feel, which it was currently. I also sought a change in places that I went to and started contacting other people and moving in other circles plus accepting offers of the past that I had not taken up in preference to where I was at that time. I quickly came to notice that all of a sudden, the recent complacency had lifted, and I started to feel more vibrant and more positive about everything around me?

That eureka moment had arrived, I started to feel the way I had wanted and thanks to you Aunty Bronwyn, I made the effort myself. It's good to hear what you say Aunty Bronwyn as it is someone from outside of your sphere, so you have no bias whatsoever and it gives you time to digest your own problems and solutions. Thank you, Aunty Bronwyn you've allowed me to change my life. Thanks Clarissa.

> *Trust is hard to come by. That's why my circle is small and tight. I'm kind of funny about making new friends.*
>
> *Eminem*

128

THOSE MYTHICAL FAMILY LINES – AN ASIAN STORY

Aunty Bronwyn Sanjay writes. Aunty Bronwyn my girlfriend got me to listen to your shows against my wishes I may add, but I'm so pleased that I did. I come from a large Asian family, one that our parents have done well. I have two brothers and a sister, we are all married. My parents started from virtually nothing and have built up a large business and not only have substantial assets but are wealthy too. They have a very nice house and eat well but are quite frugal in mentality, they could live ten times better without even being opulent or fussy, they just can't spend money, years of scrimping have curtailed the pleasure of spending anything other than on sheer necessities.

My brother has decided to come out as marrying a Christian girl, I have decided not to join the business and as for my sister she has married a relatively wealthy man and so that option for her to be a part of anything is not there anyway. As far as my brother is concerned I'm more than happy that he marries who he likes, if he is happy that's fine, he has to live with his choices as I with mine.

Our parents are beyond being up in arms, their wishes have been rejected, they have been spurned, they have been to make to look fools, we have disgraced the family, we have disgraced the community, we have brought shame on to the neighbourhood and so it goes on. To be honest Aunty Bronwyn, if I don't get a penny from them then I don't care.

I'm not prepared to live in a lie situation and suffer until they die, it's just not on. My strict parents are tea-teetotallers, and I sent them a picture of one of our parties with me having a drink and said this is my happiness, with all my friends around lifting their glasses for a "cheers" shot. Maybe not the most correct thing to do, but their reality is if they don't know it, it doesn't happen, and I don't want to be a part of that anymore. I took your saying Aunty Bronwyn, by saying if you are not happy that I'm happy then there is something wrong with you.

To date we have heard nothing whatsoever either to my brother or myself, I'm no worse off as I have to earn a living anyway as does my brother. Living within these "unofficial boundaries" and this so called "community" what does it mean? I receive nothing from any of them and I don't even know who 90% of these people are anyway, neither do I need permission from anyone to do what I need to do in life, my life is my own.

Aunty Bronwyn, just listening to your shows in particular the Asian one and the Taking Ownership one really placed deep within me my feelings towards all this made up undue and unwarranted pressure. You also did a show called "It's My Life Let Me Live It" which I had to agree with every word you spoke. Regardless of our family or who we are we are all entitled to our own lives the way we want then, we can't live our lives according to others as it is not living a life at all, we are not pets, we are human beings.

As you mention life doesn't come with a script, so we should not fall into the empty obligation mould when there is nothing to fall into.

Thank you, Aunty Bronwyn for your shows I've sent links to my friends as I think they will also benefit from them. Best wishes Sanjay.

129

BLACK AND GAY

Aunty Bronwyn Leroy writes to us. Aunty Bronwyn I'm a black young man, I think I've always known that I have been gay even before I knew what it was called. I've always had leaning towards other males whereas my peers were quite the opposite. I also noticed that I dressed better than my mates and they noticed that too, they didn't say anything but whereas they wore hoodies and baggy jeans I worse clothes that looked like clothes and not dull outsized wear for shapeless figures.

At school I was very artistic and always got good grades, even in English I did very well whereas my other compatriots spoke using about three sentences and recurring ones at that. It was at this times that I started getting a hard time, everyone was finding who they were and looked at life differently and I had an ambition, I wanted art college whereas they wanted a job of some kind and I found I had less and less in common with them. I lost most of my friends as they were embarrassed to be around me not because of me but because of who they were. When you are black you seem to have this tendency to want to "belong" whereas I wanted to be an individual because I had a mind of my own, I didn't want to be a part of some collective thinking trying to outdo each other and always failing because it never amounted to much. Also, I spoke better, and I realised that when I went anywhere I was treated better and respected because I could engage where the other guys just had a weird attitude with a rough voice that put everyone else off.

I got to art college my mum was over the moon it was more than she could have dreamed of, although she was always supportive even though she had to put up with a lot of second hand flak from many of the other women on the estate. I was openly gay to everyone at art college as if it made any difference no one cared I was there for my art not for some sex situation, that was very comforting and reassuring. I came out to my mum, until then I had kept quiet, she was a bit taken back but not surprised, yet still proud of my achievements and she was amazed that no one at college had said anything. I said it's because they are educated they understand there is more to life than who someone choses to be with or their sexual orientation.

I met other black gay students, some of whom had had a horrific time in their early teens and with their families which included violence and being bullied and ostracised by friends and family, and I really thought "good on them" for keeping going. The upshot of all of this is I got a "Distinction" in my art and am going further forward and have won a special scholarship which is only one of three offered every year.

During my term at college I actually had a very down moment, partly because of being gay and partly about where I lived, and partly because of my finances plus a number of other things that seemed to be prominent too. A friend of mine at college said she was listening to your shows Aunty Bronwyn and would I like to listen to them with her, which I said yes which in all honesty was another excuse not to go home until later just to ward off the negative feelings of my surrounding home area. Aunty Bronwyn it was magic, I wish I had heard what you had to say on just about all your topics years earlier, I was a fan from day one. You really put into perspective so much of what happens in life that we take on board yet shouldn't.

You are so right too about your upbringing and environment and I can see first- hand where many are almost born into failure because of it, I'm just so pleased that despite everything, and I don't know how I just kept going. After listening to many of your shows I had a totally different mind-set and even my mother remarked on it in a positive way and I started to boost her up, saying nothing but positive things and buying her little bits when I could afford it, and it made such a great difference to her. Being gay was no longer a problem at all as it was part of me, that's it and it's not up for discussion, in fact Aunty Bronwyn you have added so much to what I was and are that it has increased my self-esteem and humility, that life now has a new meaning.

I just want to say a big big thank you, you should be on the national curriculum it would help so many students in particular those in black areas like me. Thank you, Aunty Bronwyn big hug Leroy.

130

WHEN ANGER TAKES OVER

Aunty Bronwyn we have a letter from Sue-Ellen. Aunty Bronwyn I don't know what it is whether it was in my makeup or I had cultivated it, but I was always full on anger. Anything that went wrong, or I didn't like the anger would just have welled up inside of me and I would become animated with an internal fight. I would even start to clench my fists, make movements and start to play act a fight in my mind to appease what I thought was wrong or an injustice or even worse just to get even. The slightest little thing would set it off and then out of the blue it would re-emerge at a future time and I'd get into a frenzy re-enacting it all over again and the battle would be as real the second time around as it was the first, possibly even worse.

Anger was starting to ruin my life, I was fine as long as things were fine, but if there was a glitch no matter how small or someone did something silly even if it was inadvertent then off I would go internally living in my little word of fighting the battle. A few friends knew that I was like this, to what extent I don't know but one even said she was not inviting to me to her daughter's wedding as there would be a lot of rugby players possibly doing "laddish" things there from her husband's side and she didn't want me to suddenly launch myself into a fit of anger. I was very disappointed and a bit surprised and yes, I got angry that she had made this decision for me, but she was right because that's just what would have happened, and my friend is not a petty sort of person, she was doing what was right. I got angry again.

AUNTY BRONWYN SPEAKING TO JOHN RUSHTON

After the wedding she invited me over for a meal and asked if I wanted to see some of the wedding pictures. She also apologised for her decision not to invite me but said she valued me as a person and that "the anger thing" would have been on her mind thinking about what might have happened and as it was the day although it apparently went very well was a little stressful. I actually understood totally what she had said and because she was the person she was, I wasn't offended although I would have very much liked to have been there on the day. During the evening she mentioned your shows Aunty Bronwyn and said that there was one on Anger and Trapped Emotions and that I might want to hear it. I said I would very much because I couldn't go on the way I am, I was becoming a mess and even fearing for myself that no matter where I went I'd just flare up at the slightest little thing.

I didn't hear the Anger show straight away, but the shows I listened to all made perfect sense and were very entertaining with the family too, I had to smile a number of times. What you say Aunty Bronwyn is just as we think but don't do, and actually hearing what we think confirms to us that we should have gone with our initial instincts in the first place. It's all very enabling, it's all good to hear and it's all very cathartic in as much as you don't preach, you just say what you feel, and the listener has to make up their own mind for themselves.

It is amazing that although you have a wild array of topics and scenarios our emotions all boil down to just a few and it's just those few that we have to apply to the solutions. Your stance that "just turn the problem back upon itself" is so so true, and often when we think about the problem, which I rarely did I just flew into a rage, we can if we put our mind to it see a way out.

Often too as you mention the "biggest problem we have is ourselves" and we come in the way of a resolution because of ego and pride and our anger, I'm a classic case of that I'm sure.

I listened to the show on Anger and Trapped emotions it was really very good, it distilled many of my feelings and what I do and why. I know also that I have to work upon myself and not fuel my ego or anger I literally have to starve it of my own biased and negative thoughts because they self-perpetuate all that's bad. I have been helped a lot by your shows Aunty Bronwyn and am thankful that my friend recommended them to me I will in turn recommend them also to others who I think they will help.

Thank you, Aunty Bronwyn for your help and comments, I'm a lot calmer now, although still a way to go. All the best Sue-Ellen.

131

DON'T COMPARE YOUR LIFE – IT'S YOURS

Aunty Bronwyn we have a letter here from Annie. Aunty Bronwyn what you say about life and how we think about ourselves is so true. At times we can be our worst enemy and critic and then wonder why nothing moves in the way in which we would like. We can also have a defined view of how life could or should be for us which again may be possibly way off the mark as to how it is destined to be, and thus we forever fall into that deep pit of disappointment because nothing matches up. Whereas, there is nothing to really match up because our ideals are fabricated and not real, aligning how we think and having a reality plan is far more acceptable and plausible but it doesn't mean that at the same time we can't run with concurrent thoughts about how we would like life to be.

I had gotten into a bit of a rut which I suppose we all do at times, but in my particular case I just couldn't seem to throw it off. I even got into the habit of looking at others and hearing what others were doing and comparing it all to my current state of life and it didn't seem to add up. Your shows on Life and aspects of life really helped me look at myself and analyse what I was trying to compare, because if we are not careful we can compare unlikeable things that have no meaning other than it is just a definition of what others have done and not what you may even like to do.

Aunty Bronwyn you are so right too that when we compare we have no reference to how others life, their story, what they have been through or what they are going through all we see is the façade or as you put it the "shop window". That "shop window" effect as we all know can hide away a multitude of unhappiness and struggle and pain the likes of which we know nothing about. I know for example a good friend of mine who is always bubbly and bright has had a most horrific few years and yet to look at her and hear her you would think the opposite.

Your show on Taking Control was brilliant because it changed me from a viewer of life to a liver of life. I had to stop being a pedestrian in my own existence and start looking towards what I could do, because no one else could ever do anything or help me if I was sat viewing life from the side lines and not there to join in. It is a sobering thought process knowing that you are a part of your own problem, but it is true. As you say Aunty Bronwyn you live in your mind nowhere else and if you suddenly detach life and place it in categories then you are fragmenting your own existence. Once that happens you start to offload your own ability to change anything or do anything and then the rot sets in.

I've listened to many of your shows Aunty Bronwyn and am so grateful that you exist just to be able to put such material out there because where else could one get so much succinct information, direct without having to wade through some "Self-Help" book and be filled with smart ideas but not soluble information. Listening to you Aunty Bronwyn somehow makes it all that more plausible and workable as if it has been downloaded straight into the brain for immediate use. Everything you say is concise and complete in itself so there is no disappointment or failure it's real and honest without judgment. Thank you, Aunty Bronwyn Annie.

132

JEWISH BOY – MUSLIM GIRL – HAPPY FAMILY

Aunty Bronwyn we have a letter here from Theirry. Aunty Bronwyn I have to say I love your shows, apart from being funny at times, I've gotten used to the humour now I just love the way you go all out to speak on any subject and then just say it as it is. I know you are not politically correct and it shows but that speaks of honesty and I wouldn't trust anyone who is politically correct like the main stream media, why can't you be in charge?

I think because you have travelled the world you have seen first-hand different societies and cultures and thus have a greater understanding than the armchair fed experts who are only as good as the last message they have read. Some of life's permutations which you have outlined are way off the 'norm' but then as you say, 'what is the norm', and who has the right to say what is what?

I was at a conference in Switzerland and met this wonderful woman who was looking after our group. The moment I saw her I got that tingling feeling inside. She did too, but I didn't know that at the time and being professional and in a relatively high-powered group we just couldn't be seen to be hanging around each other all the time. I knew she was a Muslim by her name and I think she knew that I was or could have been Jewish by my last name. On the last evening when we had a buffet reception and we eventually got to talk to each other, and if there was anything called "love at first sight" that was it. That was six years ago, and we are married and have three children.

Aunty Bronwyn you should be an ambassador for humanity as you just go in there and say what needs to be said but without the negativity or bias that others have. Your shows on Taking Ownership are an epic for me because Taking Ownership is just that. It doesn't mean you won't have arguments, it doesn't mean you won't get opposition and it doesn't mean that it won't be an emotional roller coaster as you often say. What it does mean is that you Take Control and live your life according to how you want which is your right, full stop. Unravelling all the pseudo-parental, cultural, religious, indoctrination can be done in an instant. Unravelling all the pseudo-subliminal barriers and links can be unravelled in an instant too, Aunty Bronwyn you are an Angel.

The marriage between my wife and I would never ever have come about if we hadn't Taken Ownership together of our lives, I would have missed out on the greatest opportunity to meet someone ever, and why because of the stupidity of man-made selfish self-centred hypocrisy of others, all of which has nothing to do with me or my wife. The ordeal between both families was cut short in that we gave them an ultimatum like it or leave it, there was no discussion allowed because who do they think they are to discuss who I love and my wife too? Our happiness is ours if they don't like it that's fine their choice. Aunty Bronwyn you have got it so right in what you say because so many failures are because people don't live an honest love filled existence they live forever shadowed by others who have no part to play and are so selfishly motivated that the real love they have doesn't exist, it is foreshadowed by fictitious and evil ideology which has no place in life.

Your take on "love" Aunty Bronwyn is so accurate and placates all the other mumbo jumbo that people call love which they hide behind but as you rightly say they are the real failures and that's why they are never as happy as they can be. My wife's family don't talk to us, my family at a push do talk to us, neither came to the wedding which was sad, but we can put up with that because we have each other and that is the most important thing above all.

We both believe in God but tend to be "middle of the road" a sort of Christian way as that's far more stable than Judaism and especially Islam, but it's not an issue, if God is love then as a couple we are right there bang online.

Aunty Bronwyn, just to say thank you for your shows they are brilliant and for anyone who feels oppressed or put upon or whatever they feel, one listen to you and you firmly put people back on track and rightfully to be themselves. God bless Aunty Bronwyn love Theirry.

133

THE MENTAL HEALTH CONUNDRUM

Aunty Bronwyn we have a letter from Joe he writes. Aunty Bronwyn I know that one of the biggest problems generally facing many people is that of mental health, and I've enjoyed your shows on that subject too. The actual problem on how we think, and feel can be just so different, but the end result is usually the same. The sparkle and edge of living as you say is "tarnished" and one just doesn't seem to get that enjoyment or excitement of living and that in itself then causes degrees of frustration and more mind conflicts and so it goes on.

I have to say Aunty Bronwyn that after listening to many of your shows I really feel a lot better about myself and life. You often say it is the smallest of things at times that can made a big difference "small pin bursting a big balloon" and that is so true. Much of mental health is not the of a clinical type condition but how we process the information we have and then how we assimilate it often hiding behind "stuff" we have created ourselves to try and absolve ourselves of doing things or as you say Aunty Bronwyn the "blame culture" thing. Never my fault always someone else's or circumstances none of which holds any water whatsoever. You are right too that if we are glum and feeling out of it those around us move away which compounds how we feel as if they don't have problems too and are not going to hang around those who do nothing to help themselves.

I listened to some of your shows recently on Q&A where listeners had written in with questions and your answers were just so simple and very short indeed, and in reality, it is all about Taking Ownership nothing more. It doesn't have to be drastic but complaining that people treat you badly or put upon you it is because you let them.

There are ways and means of getting around that but blaming others isn't going to do anything and I used to be one of those people. I used to have a negative view of life and sure enough I wallowed in negativity to the extent that I created a negative world. It has changed substantially, and it has made such a difference and that I can "let go" too of stuff which isn't important instead of churning it over in my mind".

It is funny you hear saying such as "life is what you make it" and it is like water off a duck's back, because it appears too simple and it stops you getting the attentions for your own problems which you long for to reiterate how bad the world is towards you. What a load of twaddle that is, it is you who can change everything, maybe not quite how you would like never the less you can change it and if you rightly don't respect yourself and your self-esteem is low then it is never going to happen.

It's a shame that your shows aren't available more openly for people to listen to as I really think it would give many that impetus to just do something as it did me. You are right Aunty Bronwyn when you dwell on problems you never see the solutions and you never see the endless opportunities that abound, they all fly by to those who are receptive to them. It's also true that no one likes whingers and moaners and those that feel sorry for themselves, why should they, I know I have been there.

Thank you, Aunty Bronwyn for your shows they have been a real tonic for me. All the best. Joe.

134

I LIKE BEING SINGLE

Aunty Bronwyn we have a letter from Isabel who writes. Aunty Bronwyn I'm in my mid 50's and I'm single and I like it very much. It seems to go against the grain these days as to being single and a "cranky spinster" as it were, but I really like where I am in life. I've had relationships in my past and for one reason or another they have just fizzled out. I'm sure that there were reasons beyond what I know, but they are in the past now and life is what it is.

I have been a fan of yours for some time and what you say makes sense, I feel quite satisfied after listening in to your shows whereas other shows I've felt a little frustrated because there was too much waffle and not enough concrete stuff said. Even though I say I'm happy, on my own which I am, I still at times have that feeling that maybe I could have someone else in my life, but that soon dissipated. On listening to what you have had to say on many of the shows it really brought home to my who I am as a person, and that I really don't have to keep questioning myself about why I'm here or could I or should I as that doesn't give myself any peace.

I now feel quite at ease with myself, I have a good circle of friends and am always out and have people around to see me so I'm busy and it's nice to know that genuinely people phone me, call on me and invite me out too. You are write Aunty Bronwyn, that life is holistic in that there is a need for reciprocation of a certain kind, you have to give of yourself because if you don't it all goes so sour and then comes to a halt. You also have to accept that everyone is not going to be to your liking too and possibly you not to theirs so one has to be compassionate to others.

I know all the talks today are to find partners, but I just can't see myself with one at all. I'm too much of a "me" person, yet I love mixing with my friends and never put off any opportunity to go out with them. Thank you for your shows Aunty Bronwyn, they really do make sense, and some are just so funny with the family. Best wishes Isabel.

Thousands of candles can be lighted from a single candle, and the life of the candle will not be shortened. Happiness never decreases by being shared.

Buddha

135

I AM SOCIETY

Aunty Bronwyn we have a letter from Jarrod. Aunty Bronwyn I was captivated by what you had to say to a number of people in your recent Q&A session in response to their questions. You were of course right that we are everyone of us part of society and for people to say "well that's society today" obfuscates the situation and excludes the self, which is not on and is not true. It was amazing really how many people get themselves lost and tied up in what they deem life is all about, many getting it so terribly wrong.

Your direct approach at times is just that Aunty Bronwyn, but I've never heard you be rude to anyone, you tell it as it is and for that I think you are head and shoulders above all others I have heard talking about aspects of life or even social commentating. I was listening to one of your general shows where people just ask questions and you said very clearly "what do you want to happen" so that your life will change for the better? There was a silence, so you said, 'well that says it all', you have to make an effort and do it yourself or change your goals because no one can alter your life but you. It actually hit me too because I was if I have to be honest one who thought because of this or that I can't move forward as I want but I now realise that such conversation doesn't exist except within your mind. If you want to do something, then it is up to you to do it.

I think in one fell swoop I had stopped being a listener and now I was a participant in the conversations, I too was a victim of my own mind set, I too was a culprit of my own thoughts and I actually thought I was quite broadminded but in reality, I was as broadminded as I allowed myself to be and no more.

It is strange when you are confronted with what you think is a comfort zone within yourself yet in reality you say one thing and think or do another and live with that dichotomy. Reality is such a sobering thing yet at the same time it is so liberating too because then nothing holds you back at all, everything is possible if it means that much to you.

Thank you, Aunty Bronwyn for your shows I think they are now liberating in that they are more than just answers or common-sense solutions, they can really free you up from yourself and your self-deceptions. All the best Jarrod.

> *Nothing in life is to be feared,*
> *it is only to be understood.*
> *Now is the time to understand more,*
> *so that we may fear less.*
>
> *Marie Curie*

136

THE POWER OF LOVE - DISOWNMENT

Aunty Bronwyn Beth writes to us. Aunty Bronwyn I love your shows they are so enlightening, and I have to admit a bit scary too in that facing your own gremlins is a bit of a challenge, but once done you are freed from all the detritus of life and media and everything else which has been stuffed down your throat. One of your shows on love was unusual in that it confronted the depth and the meaning of love and what we think we understand or inherently know and what is possibly the reality of it not being as we expected.

You have had a number of people giving their account of their parents turning them out or disowning their children because their children did not conform to what was required. It was all very sad that the love that was there was in reality conditional and nothing more. The people who had had mixed marriages, inter-faith marriages, announced they were gay, etc, and suddenly the parents didn't want to know them. How sad and devastating that is and what kind of parents are these people to bring someone into this world to denounce them for being happy it was so very sad and so very emotional.

The kindness of some parents is almost stripped away by the callousness of others, but it doesn't stop there the emotional hurt that these people suffer purely through the selfishness of others. The price for being happy results in being disowned whilst the price for unhappiness is the opposite. What kind of society and people are there who do this? I was orphaned at an early age because my parents both died in an accident and they were of European stock so neither had other family close by. I was so lucky that I was adopted by wonderful people who are my parents now, they have done everything for me and I know I'm lucky when I hear these sad stories of disownment.

Aunty Bronwyn I know there is nothing to say about such pathetic and sad people inflicting disownment upon others, but I think the fact that it has been highlighted gives those disowned a degree of hope that they are not alone in this sad world at times and that love does exist. Real love always finds a way, one way or another and real love is always worth it, always, there's never a shadow of doubt about it.

Thank you, Aunty Bronwyn for your shows they are always an inspiration even if at times you deal with some tough subjects you deal with them so well that you realise that there are always solutions even if your eyes at times are full of tears. You are so right that it is often our own ignorance that makes us think that solutions are going to be complicated and hurtful and stressful and everything else whereas it's just one little change here and a slightly different thought position here and bingo you are already on the road to a massive change that has positive repercussions.

Thank you, Aunty Bronwyn. Beth.

137

BREAKING FREE – A GIRL'S STORY

We have a letter from Julia Aunty Bronwyn she writes. Aunty Bronwyn the first time I heard your shows I thought this is for me, you are so different, and I've always been different not by design but by default all my life. As a child I was a bit of a loner not because I didn't mix or didn't like other children, but I found I had little in common with them, so I wasn't in a position to be interested in what they did. It was a strange childhood and on reflection it caused my parents a degree of consternation because I wouldn't fit in. I realised this was a shortcoming on their side, but I suppose it was their narrow upbringing too that made them feel insecure or helpless in such a situation.

I did quite well at school, but I was always the odd one out although I didn't realise that because it was me being me. My brother on the other hand was the "normal" one who played with all the other boys and was sporty and all the rest. When I was at school some of the teachers would ask me why I did what I did, and I didn't have a clue as to what they were talking about which some understood, and others got annoyed about as if I was being awkward, but I wasn't. One of the girls two grades higher than me lived not far away and we sometimes walked home together. One day she said you are quite creative in your appearance which was the first complement I had ever had. She was also very creative, and I had meant to say the same to her but never got around to it. She was the next term about to leave and go to art college to study textile design and asked if I wanted to come around after school to see her collection and portfolio.

I dashed home, ate then got ready, my mother was beside herself about how I looked and said you can't go out like that, but I did. I went to my friends and she loved how I looked and said I ought to try for art college when the time is right. It was an evening to remember the first time I had been appreciated and understood, and it really made me feel that I am on the right lines even if everyone else can't get to terms with it. Your shows, Aunty Bronwyn, are just so inspirational in that without any judgment you just say always be yourself never ever be the thought of someone else, ever. Despite my local world being at odds with me, just you Aunty Bronwyn and my friend understood, and that's all the recognition I needed at least for then.

I got into college, my parents were pleased but apprehensive as to how I would turn out, when I went home they would just stare at me as if to say where did we go wrong, but now I was used to life's philistines and how ignorance can take a hold of people and even give them a fear perspective when in reality it's nothing to do with anyone else.

I subsequently graduated, and on my graduation a French lady was viewing my collection and asked me if I would be interested to work for a term in France as a junior designer. A move I couldn't refuse, the experience was invaluable not least that I was taking a degree of British quirkiness with me which went down a storm. How I dressed doesn't exist as such in France, and I was always the centre of attention in a good way. My term with the fashion house came up for renewal and I was asked if I would like to stay on, I declined as I needed to go further so returned to the UK.

I now have my own small fashion label. I love each day despite the unstable and highly competitive nature of the industry it's me through and through. Aunty Bronwyn you must give so many people hope where hope is in short supply. There are, and I've seen it so many young people ignored because they don't fit in with the dull and narrow understanding of life and those in the educational system. Entrepreneurs don't exist in education, creativity in particular at the lower levels is actually frowned upon, conformity is more the norm than individuality, and government ministers play at the "one size fits all" as you so often say Aunty Bronwyn, they understand statistics and rhetoric but nothing more.

Thank you, Aunty Bronwyn for what you do, it can be hard out there when you are fighting your own battles in unchartered territory especially when young. Just listening to you really gave me the confidence to at least have a go if not wholeheartedly pursue my dreams, and today it has worked. God bless you Aunty Bronwyn and a big thank you. Julia.

138

TOY BOY OR TRUE LOVE?

Aunty Bronwyn we have a letter from Tony. Aunty Bronwyn there's a lot said about toy boys and toy girls or girls with rich 'daddies' and I'm not sure whether it is true or not only that what has happened to me has happened without any planned motive. Your show on "Toy Boys" rang so true and you were wonderful Aunty Bronwyn for just allowing the free flow of conversation to happen without judgment or induced scepticism or cynicism.

From an early age I've always had this thing for the "older" woman, I don't know why but my mum's friends who used to come around were always that much more attractive than my sister's friends. I think I liked the maturity in that they had been through life already and could both enjoy and laugh at silly things but know the difference between being silly and blatant ignorance. I also liked sophisticated things, the general etiquette of life it really fascinated me whereas people my own age were generally just "green around the gills" about these things. I could go on because the "mature" aspect just had it hands down for me every time, it won me over and the more sophisticated a woman was the more I really fell for them – as well as the looks of course.

I would go as far to say that my down time, the quiet moments, the moments of just chilling out etc my thoughts were focussed on the more mature woman who was far more assured in general because she knew what she liked or wanted whereas girls my own age just tended to do whatever they found interesting to "chill out", but it overall held no passion at all for them.

Another point was that conversations rarely included celebrity gossip I know this can vary from person to person buy younger people tend to be more wrapped up in it and I can't stand nor even care about any of it.

I have been in a relationship with a woman, 20 years older than myself, and we have been together now for six years and I love every moment of it. We just clicked from day one, it was strange because neither of us had thought of such a relationship but over a short time it developed from a couple of meetings per week to daily meetings then moving in. Financially, we are both independent and as yet have had to have an argument over money or indeed anything else. We both agree at times that we have a different view on things but that we understand is often down to experience and so it is "live and let live" and we agree to differ but not fall out and that's the important thing.

Aunty Bronwyn, we both listen to your shows they are really great and in many ways they have helped us even come closer because we discuss some of the topics afterwards, and that's always interesting because we see at times different perspectives, all of which are feasible and plausible. Like you keep saying Aunty Bronwyn, there isn't such a thing as "one size fits all".

I'm sure that there are couples whereby there is a wealthy woman and a good looking young male partner, the "token" "hot guy" or vice versa, the trophy but that happens everywhere in all walks in life. The bottom line in any relationship must be love otherwise the relationship will turn into an endurance and then it will be held together only by appearances and that's not even an excuse for anything.

AUNTY BRONWYN SPEAKING TO JOHN RUSHTON

It will all start to crumble and lots of animosity will creep into both their lives and again you only get out what you put in.

Thank you for your excellent show Aunty Bronwyn, it was so very interesting to hear we both thoroughly enjoyed it. Best Wishes Tony.

> ***I'm not just a boy toy.***
> ***I have feelings and dreams***
> ***like anybody else.***
>
> ***Jon Stewart***

139

"DAUGHTERS" AND "DADDIES" – YOUNG GIRL AND OLDER MAN

Aunty Bronwyn we have a letter from Samantha who writes. Aunty Bronwyn I listened to your show on "Toy Boy or True Love" and it was very good indeed, I agreed with everything that was said and you keep it so well balanced and in perspective, out of the clutches of media smearing. I was hoping you would have a similar one for girls who have fallen for older men or vice versa. Like in your previous show I was always fascinated with older men, my dad's friends always seemed far more interesting than boy's my age and I loved the sophistication and knowledge they had too, it was all a big sexy plus point whichever way you looked at it.

I have to admit that it was not that easy going out with men quite a bit senior not because of what others had to say but it was at times their "trophy" and I didn't need that, and as much as I like nice meals etc, I didn't just need wining and dining with that hope it was an entre for sex later, it wasn't. All the men I went with were previously married and now divorced, I think all of them had had a bad divorce too by the sound of it, as none of them spoke well at all of their previous relationships – there seemed to be a common pattern but I'm not sure as to how it all came about.

One of the main causes of these more "mature" men wanting a younger partner – from what I had gleaned - was that their previous wives had seemed to have lost the sparkle, many just wanting to be kept at a certain "lifestyle" but offer nothing in return. It all seemed to have become dull and soured with little joint excitement or interests to keep the relationship working.

They had ended up as almost two people living together in the same building and nothing more. This then obviously caused great friction and the rest all becomes history.

I have found a great man Aunty Bronwyn, he's not wealthy and has to still work, however we have hit it off with so much in common that even my life which was good before is just fun packed all the time. He makes time for me, we go out all over the place, we have our mutual friends, and whilst he is proud of me and I of him, we never show off each other because we don't have to. I love cooking as does he and we entertain often which is great fun and try all kinds of different foods. Aunty Bronwyn, it is wonderful, there is nearly a 30-year difference between us but to us it is just a number nothing more. I have a good job and don't rely on him for any financial income although he is considerate in that direction, but I know his financial status, so I would hate for him to be generous for the sake of it and then suffer. We have to be reasonable and make this relationship work.

If we are to be honest, whatever life we have together we need to treasure right now, tomorrow is ticking away for us, although none of us know what is around the corner. Whatever years we have they need to be enjoyed to the full and I am aware that the fun we do have is excellent, I'm so happy. The bulk of his estate goes to his children and they know that, and I have some small legacy which he has made openly aware to the children and myself and everyone is happy.

His children were a little apprehensive when we first met, was I a gold digger, was I this n' that. Was I, you name it, I could have been it, but since the Will has been made everything is really cool and they have even said that they have never seen their father so bubbly. Of course, I'm biased but Aunty Bronwyn I just wanted to say your programmes are so diverse and so real they are something to behold. It is so good to just listen to others and what everyone has had to go through to get where they are. Relationships no matter what need work, no excuses if you don't work at them they will fail that's for sure.

Thank you, Aunty Bronwyn again for your shows. Fond regards Samantha.

> *You don't get older, you get better.*
>
> **Shirley Bassey**

140

DON'T BE AFRAID TO DISAPPOINT

Aunty Bronwyn we have a letter from Karl. Aunty Bronwyn I have to say you are so good at apportioning emotions in the correct way because we are brought up in such a way that the word failure is almost ingrained within us somewhere. We like to please because it pleases us, it's almost the same reciprocal emotion and if we don't please we are almost automatically ourselves not pleased. But Aunty Bronwyn you are so right, if we do everything we can, and it doesn't please others we can feel guilty because of that. However, it boils down to expectations in that we can give a 110% and still be wrong, so there is no need to feel guilty whatsoever. In fact, the person judging us can be the one at fault indeed they can be unstable and selfish and self-centred and greedy so whatever we do they could still want more.

I had a very domineering mother who was never satisfied with anything I did, she would always complain always put me down, always mutter something about how she could never rely on me and this when you are growing up has an effect upon you. As I got older and did things for other people and they really liked what I had done I realised that it may just not be me it could be my mother's problem.

I eventually moved out of the house and got a flat of my own, but the past still haunted me, all those negative years that kept unappeased at the back of my mind.

I was listening to your shows and the one on Taking Ownership just struck a chord, you said "turn your problem back on to itself". I wasn't sure what I was going to do, but I felt confident that I would do something. On a visit back home, my mother launched into one of her failure speeches and I just exploded. I told her she was the biggest failure in my life, the worst selfish mother on the planet, and she has as much compassion as a lump of ice, I said I've never heard you say one nice thing to me there's something wrong with you. She was completely taken back, stunned in fact, but at that I left, I couldn't bear what was to follow and I was too shaken up myself to do or say anything. Why did this always have to happen?

Whatever had happened had worked, it took me a couple of days to calm down and I also felt guilty at having a go but at the same time I felt I was right to have eventually said it all. My mother eventually phoned, and I could tell that the "superior" voice she had used to dominate the conversation had left her she was indeed frightened at what I may have said further. The conversation went through the usual how are you etc, and then she apologised in her own way for her attitude of the past. She came out with the story of her mother, but I cut her short and said, perhaps your past had an influence but what you did was still deliberate don't hide behind that fact.

A bit of crying on the phone from her but I held my own stance and just kept silent waiting for her to make the next move, which she eventually did. She agreed it was her and she unreservedly apologised for the past and hoped that I would still come to see her and that I meant everything to her, the first time I'd ever heard anything like that.

Aunty Bronwyn, I'm not sure if I went the right way about what I did, but it was my way and the upshot of it all was it worked.

I do at long last have a loving mother on the outside as well as on the inside. I can't complain about how I was treated or looked after at all, but it is so important that how we all talk to one another is good and wholesome, it really is. Looking after people mentally is as important as the physical side of things.

Thank you, Aunty Bronwyn for your shows they have helped me very much and I'm sure many others too. Best wishes Karl.

Daring to set boundaries is about having the courage to love ourselves, even when we risk disappointing others.

Brene Brown

END CHAPTER

The chapters you have just read on the various letters depicting scenarios and events that have happened to readers and how they have coped with or rectified the situations at hand are just a few of those sent to us. These are not isolated cases, and many of you will have found possibly a number of areas that resonated well within yourself.

What does come to light very easily is that in most cases we have to adjust very little to effect big changes, often it's the same change that affects many other areas in our lives at the same time. We don't have a string or succession of little things to do, as just a few encompass many areas and greatly improve our lives and perspective.

We also see that much of the fogginess that comes over us and clouds our decisions is self-created. This "what will others think", is us giving away our authority no matter who the others are as if they (there is) some great authority over us and we need their permission, in reality there is nothing of the sort.

This book in conjunction with the Radio Broadcasts is the first in a series of books and Audio Downloads highlighting very real situations in life giving comfort and solace to those who have experienced emotional conditions which have been either hindering their own way forward or causing degrees of consternation.

Within the letters there have been solutions, however there is not a "one size fits all" even if the advice is sage advice, we all have different thoughts and parameters and thus how we deal with our own problems is down to us.

I sincerely hoped you enjoyed reading the letters in this book and am always interested to hear your own views in life and how you came through them.

With love

Aunty Bronwyn.....

AUNTY BRONWYN PRODUCTIONS
"Sound Advice"

www.auntybronwyn.com

Available on :-

iPad
iPhone
iTunes
Phone
Android
Tablet
PC
Mac
Radio
Internet
Books
Downloads
YouTube
Facebook
Twitter
Video

Aunty Bronwyn is there for you wherever you are....

©Aunty Bronwyn Productions
2013/2025

AUNTY BRONWYN SPEAKING TO JOHN RUSHTON

www.ingramcontent.com/pod-product-compliance
Lightning Source LLC
Chambersburg PA
CBHW061227070526
44584CB00029B/4024